Pathways

to

Academic English

2021

Institute for Excellence in Higher Education, Tohoku University

Tohoku University Press, Sendai

本教材に関する情報、英語学習に役立つ情報を配布しますので、

Pathways to Academic English 2021 を購入したら、下記の QR コードを利用

して、学籍番号を入力してください

Pathways to Academic English 2021

Table of Contents

English B2: Integrated Academic Speaking and Listening

1. *Develop pragmatic competence*

2. *Acquire the ability to discuss various topics*

English C: Integrated Writing and Presentation

1. *Acquire the ability to write an academic essay*

2. *Acquire the ability to create and give an academic presentation*

序文

研究大学である東北大学では、学部を問わず、working language（共通使用言語）として英語が使われています。したがって、学生の皆さんは専門領域の知識や教養を身に付ける際、英語を通じて知識を取り入れ、英語を使って考察・発表・執筆する機会を持つこととなります。このような学術目的の英語の土台を作るために提供されるのが、全学教育として英語科目（1・2年次）です。

本書は、2021年度の入学生向け英語カリキュラムに準拠した共通教材として、学術英語の土台として必要な Core Skills を解説したものです。1年次では4つの英語科目（「英語 A1」「英語 B1」「英語 A2」「英語 B2」）を履修することになりますが、各科目には Core Skills が4つずつ配置されています。担当教員は、この4つの Core Skills を全て取り入れた授業を行い、学生が本書の内容を習得できるよう練習を重ねます。2年次では、1年次で学習した16の Core Skills を踏まえて、さらに4つの Core Skills を英語科目「英語 C1」と「英語 C2」で学習します。

これらの Core Skills が、学部高年次における専門科目や大学院での本格的な研究に従事する際の一般的基礎力となるので、手を抜くことなく英語力の一層の向上に励んでください。また、本書に収められた20の Core Skills は学術目的ですが、将来の活躍の場所を官公庁や企業、あるいは起業に求める人にとっても有益なスキルとなるでしょう。なぜなら、どのような進路を選ぶにしても、それぞれの分野における専門性を身に付けることが求められるからです。

本書はこの「序文」を除き、すべて英語で書かれていますが、これには理由があります。すでに述べたとおり、英語を通じて専門分野の知識や幅広い教養を身に付けていくことが、これから皆さんに求められる英語との付き合い方です。したがって、学術目的の英語力を身に付けるのも英語を通じて行ってほしいと願うからです。実際、本学では多くの英語科目が英語で実施されることになるでしょう。

英語は履修科目の1つというよりは、研究・学習のための道具であり環境です。学生の皆さんがすでに習得している英語力を活性化させ、英語を working language として使えるようになるよう、本書がその一助となることを願ってやみません。

English A1

Academic Reading and Vocabulary

Objective 1: Improve reading and vocabulary-building skills

A1.1 Word Parts
A1.2 Synonym Vocabulary

Objective 2: Acquire the ability to quickly recognize the text's main idea and key information

A1.3 Skimming and Scanning
A1.4 Summarizing and Paraphrasing

A1.1 Word Parts

Learning English word parts is a very effective way to build vocabulary. There are three basic components of many English words: prefixes, roots and suffixes. An English word may contain any combination or number of each of these three parts—or none at all; however, the prefix-root-suffix pattern is common. Over half of English words have prefixes, roots and suffixes that are borrowed from the Latin and Greek languages. In addition, most English technical, academic, scientific and medical vocabulary words are constructed using Latin and Greek. Recognizing word parts helps students when reading, writing or being examined on academic, scientific or medical subjects because it provides clues to the meanings of words. In addition, it helps students remember difficult vocabulary more easily.

What to Know About Word Parts

For many complex historical and linguistic reasons, English adopted word parts from Latin and Greek. For example, when a certain electrical communication device was invented in the mid-19th century that allowed people to talk to one another at a distance, the Greek words *tele* (distant) and *phone* (sound) were combined to create the new English word "telephone." The first step to mastering word parts is to know how English vocabulary words are "built" using Latin and Greek. Therefore, it is important to develop the ability to recognize the function of each word part.

Prefixes
Prefixes come at the beginning of a word. Two common English prefixes are *multi*, from Latin, and *poly,* from Greek. Both mean "many," but they are used for different functions. Some meanings can be very straightforward, while others are not. For example, the adjective "multicultural" simply means "relating to many cultures." On the other hand, the noun "polytypic" does not mean "many types," but "more than one type." Knowing the meaning of prefixes like these is a powerful vocabulary tool.

Roots
To illustrate how roots work in the English language, we can examine the Greek root *nêsos*, meaning "island." From this root come several commonplace English place names, namely, "Polynesia" (many-island-place), "Micronesia" (small-island-place) and Melanesia (black-island-place). Interestingly, these words also occur in Japanese as *porineshia, mikuroneshia* and *meraneshia*. This example demonstrates that Japanese university students can not only improve their English vocabulary but also better understand Japanese foreign loan words if they familiarize themselves with Latin and Greek word parts. It also demonstrates that words such as

these are not just random sounds but have distinctive meanings and therefore can be more easily retained.

Suffixes

Often suffixes do not have actual meanings but instead indicate grammatical functions. They can determine parts of speech (nouns, verbs, adjectives, etc.), grammatical tenses, plurals and the comparative and superlative word forms. For example, the English adjective, "polytheistic"—constructed by using the Greek prefix, *poly*, the Greek root, *theos* (God) and the hybrid suffix, *ic* (forms adjectives)—means, "relating to the belief in many gods." Changing the suffix alters the grammatical function of the word. For example, "polytheism" is a noun that means "the belief in many gods." "Polytheist," also a noun, means "a person who believes in many gods." Understanding suffixes in this way is essential to mastering academic English grammar.

Charts of Important Word Parts

Students should memorize many of the Latin and Greek prefixes, roots and suffixes, particularly those found in the charts of the most commonly occurring word parts below. Since these charts are not complete, medical, science and engineering majors, especially, should refer to free, online Latin and Greek to English and Japanese dictionaries.

Common Prefixes

Latin	Greek	Meanings	Example Vocabulary
at-		towards	attract, attempt
co-	syn-	with	cooperate, synchronize
contra-	anti-	against, opposing	contradiction, antisocial
de-		removing	deforest, defrost
dom-	eco-	home	domestic, ecosystem
en-/em-		adding, entering	entrap, empower
ex-		out, former	exit, extract
in-/im-/il-/ir-	dis-	not, non	injustice, disagree
inter-		between	international, intercept
mal-	mis-	wrong, bad, sick	malaria, misunderstand
max-	macro-	large	maximum, macroeconomics
mini-	micro-	small	miniskirt, microscope
multi-	poly-	many	polyglot, multimedia
non-		without	nontoxic, nonsense
over-	hyper-	too much	overeat, hypertension
post-		after	postscript, postmodern
pre-		before	predict, preview

pro-		forward, giving	promote, provide
re-		back, again	reuse, retreat
semi-		half, partial	semicircle, semipro
sub-		under	subway, subconscious
super-	acro-	over	superior, acrobat
uni-	mono-	one	monopoly, uniform
	auto-	self	automatic, autograph
un-		without	unclean, unthinkable
out-		doing better	outthink, outrun

Common Roots

Latin	Greek	Meanings	Example Vocabulary
bi	du	two	bicycle, duet
tri		three	tricycle, triangle
qua(r)t	tetra	four	quarter, tetrapod
quin	pent	five	quintuplet, pentagon
anim	bio	living	animal, biological
aqua	hydro	water	aquatic, hydrogen
astro		star	asterisk, astronaut
capt/cept		catch	capture, intercept
circum	peri	around	circumstance, perimeter
corp	phys	body	corpse, physical, physician
cred		believe	credit card, incredible
dict		Say, word	dictionary, predict
duc)t)		guide, gather	conduct, produce
dur		continue, endure	duration, durable
equ	homo	same	equal, homogeneous
flect(x)		bend	flexible, reflect
form	morph	shape	uniform, metamorphosis
gress	amb(u)l	walk	progress, ambulance
herb	botan	plant	herbicide, botany
homin	anthrop	human	hominoid, anthropology
ign-	pyr	fire	ignite, pyrophoric
ject		throw	object, eject
lact		milk	lactate, lactic acid
ling/lang		tongue, language	bilingual, language
loc		place, position	location, local

lum(in)	phot	light	illumination, photosynthesis
ment	psycho	mind, soul	mental, psychology
mort	necr	death	mortal, necrophobia
nov	neo	new	novel, innovate, neoliberal
omni	pan	all	omnibus, panorama
pel		pull	repel, expel
pend		hang	depend, suspend
port		carry	portable, export
rupt		break	rupture, erupt
sci	cogn	knowledge	science, cognition, conscious
scribe / script	graph	record, write	prescribe, graphic
sol	heli	sun	parasol, helium
sol		alone	solo, desolate
son	phon	sound	sonic, phonology
spec		look, characteristic	special, inspect
struct		build	structure, construct
tempor	chron	time	temporal, chronological
terr	geo	ground, earth	territory, geography
tox		poison	toxic, detoxify
tract		pull	tractor, distract
trans	meta	change, across	translate, metaphor
vac		empty	vacant, evacuate
vert		turn, change	vertical, convert, invert
vis	scope	see	visual, microscope
vo(u)r		eat	herbivore, devour
	agri	field	agriculture, agribusiness
	gen	birth, type	generate, genre
	hemo	blood	hemoglobin, hemorrhage
	hetero	different	heterogeneous, heterosexual
	log	study, reasoning	logic, biology
	meter	measure	metric, kilometer
	nat	birth	natal, natural
	path	suffering, feeling	pathology, sympathy, pathetic
	ped/pod	foot	pedal, tripod
	pharm	drug	pharmacy, pharmaceutical
	tele	afar	telescope, telephone
	therm	heat	thermometer, thermal

Common Suffixes

Suffix	Attaches to a	Forms a	Meanings	Example Vocabulary
-ate	noun	verb	to do (∼)	facilitate, accentuate
-en	adjective		make (∼)	sweeten, brighten
-ify	adjective		make (∼)	purify, solidify
-ize	noun/adj		to do (∼)	prioritize, summarize, finalize
-ance	verb	Noun	the action of (∼)	performance, allowance
-(m)ent	verb		the effect of doing (∼)	entertainment, government
-(t)ion	verb		the result of doing (∼)	imagination, succession
-ant	verb		person doing (∼)	assistant, immigrant
-er/-or	verb		person doing (∼)	teacher, operator
-ist	noun		person doing (∼)	guitarist, nutritionist
-oid	noun		the shape of (∼)	humanoid, android
-ness	adjective		the degree of (∼)	darkness, sweetness
-ity	various		the degree of (∼)	acidity, ability
-hood	various		time/place of (∼)	childhood, neighborhood
-ism	various		theory of (∼)	pacifism, optimism
-phile	various		person loving (∼)	anglophile, xenophile
-phobe	various		person who fears (∼)	xenophobe, technophobe
-phobia	various		condition of fearing (∼)	acrophobia, hydrophobia
-able	verbs	adjective	can do (∼)	enjoyable, readable
-al	noun		characteristic of (∼)	judgmental, experimental
-ic	noun			historic, heroic
-y	noun			windy, dirty
-ous	noun			poisonous, famous
-ive	noun		function/tendency of (∼)	expensive, supportive
-ese/-an	noun		originated from (∼)	Japanese, Mexican
-ful	noun		characterized by (∼)	eventful, forgetful
-less	noun		without (∼)	careless, sugarless
-ish	noun		like / belonging to (∼)	childish, boyish
-ly	adjective	adverb	the way of / do like (∼)	wisely, colorfully, hopelessly

Example of Word Parts in Use

For each <u>underlined</u> word, choose the most appropriate definition by referring to the Latin and Greek prefix, root and suffix charts above.

1) <u>Periscope</u>
   (A) a device used in medicine
   (B) a device for a mobile telephone
   (C) a device that enables the surroundings to be seen in 360 degrees
   (D) a device that enables the surroundings to be seen periodically

2) <u>Android</u>
   (A) a type of mobile telephone
   (B) a kind of software
   (C) a general communication device
   (D) a human-like robot

3) <u>Phonology</u>
   (A) a device that plays recorded sounds
   (B) the study of language sounds
   (C) the study of light
   (D) a type of pathology

4) <u>Phonograph</u>
   (A) a device that plays recorded sounds
   (B) the study of language sounds
   (C) the study of light
   (D) a device that measures graphite

5) <u>Subterranean</u>
   (A) underground
   (B) underwater
   (C) through ground
   (D) through water

The answer to question 1 is "C" because *peri* = "around" and *scope* = "see."
The answer to question 2 is "D" because *andro* = "human" and *oid* = "shape."
The answer to question 3 is "B" because *phono* = "sound" and *log* = "study."
The answer to question 4 is "A" because *phono* = "sound" and *graph* = "record."
The answer to question 5 is "A" because *sub* = "under" and *terr* = "ground."

A1.2 Synonym Vocabulary

A synonym is a word or phrase that has exactly or nearly the same meaning as another word or phrase. A wider knowledge of synonyms can help students understand and use English more fluently. In academic writing, synonyms enable writers to express ideas clearly, precisely, and with the proper nuance. Furthermore, knowledge of synonym vocabulary is necessary for writing with variety, when paraphrasing and summarizing (see Chapter A1.4), and to understand texts and speech. Therefore, learning synonym vocabulary will help you to increase your proficiency in all four language skills as well as be useful when writing reports and taking tests at Tohoku University.

What to Know about Synonym Vocabulary

One of the best ways to improve synonym vocabulary is to stop relying on English-Japanese dictionaries, and instead use English dictionaries or thesauruses when looking up the meanings of new words. However, there are five clues that you can use to help you guess the meanings of vocabulary words, think of synonyms for paraphrasing and variety, and expand your synonym vocabulary without using a dictionary: illustrative phrases, word parts and word families, context, denotative and connotative meanings, and collocations.

Illustrative Phrases

Illustrative phrases are sets of words that introduce the same ideas for simplicity, contrast or emphasis. When an illustrative phrase is used, you can use the surrounding words to guess that an unknown word will probably have a similar or opposite meaning. Below are some words that signal such illustrative phrases.

> *For words with similar meanings*: for example, such as, that is to say, in other words
> *For words with opposite meanings*: as opposed to, in contrast, contrary to

For example, consider the sentence: "Sadly, the community was terribly impoverished without even basic services, **that is to say**, the people were <u>destitute</u>." In this sentence, you can guess that "destitute" means the same as "impoverished," which includes the idea that they "don't have basic services," and leads you to the understanding that "destitute" means "poor." For another example, consider the sentence: "He was a handsome and <u>charismatic</u> man, **as opposed to** his brother who was ugly and boring." In this sentence, you can guess that "charismatic" has the opposite meaning of "boring," because it shows two positive traits about one man and two exactly opposite negative traits of his brother. Since "ugly" matches as the opposite of "handsome," "boring" must be used here as the opposite of "charismatic." Notice that both of these sentences contain illustrative phrase markers (in **bold**), as listed above.

Word Parts and Word Families

Word parts can be helpful when trying to understand how close two words match as synonyms, and also to think of new synonyms for academic writing. First, in order to help determine the meanings of words and identify proper synonyms for them, you can break them down into word parts (See Chapter A1.1). By identifying prefixes, roots or suffixes, you can clarify the meaning of words, and sometimes find the feeling behind a word. For example, the word "reject" contains the word parts "re-" (back) and "ject" (to throw). Though in modern English "reject" often does not mean to literally throw something back, it can help you understand that *"rejecting a job application"* is a somewhat strong expression, because it originates from these word parts. Next, when trying to think of a different word when writing, either for variety or to paraphrase, you can sometimes find new words with the same meaning simply by replacing Latinate word parts with Greek word parts, English words or vice-versa. For example, if you want to think of a synonym for "unbelievable" you might recall that "in-" is the Latinate word part for "not" and "cred" is the Latinate word part for "believe" or "trust," and you could then think of the word "incredible."

Another way that word parts can be used to find or understand synonyms is through word families – groups of words that contain the same root and basic meaning, but different suffixes or prefixes. For example, consider the word family for "consist."

consist

consistency   consistent   consistently   inconsistent   inconsistency   inconsistently

If you know the above word family and are trying to think of a different way to say "this sample is not consistent," you can quickly think of phrases using words from the same word family such as "this sample is inconsistent," "this sample lacks consistency," or "this sample contains inconsistencies." Even though "consistent" is an adjective and "consistency" is a noun, if you have mastered word parts, you should be able to recognize the part of speech easily and form a sentence or phrase that is grammatically correct for the word that you are using.

Context

Even if two words can be used as synonyms, they cannot always be used as synonyms in every situation. One reason for this is that some words have multiple meanings (e.g. "great" can mean both "big" and "good"). Therefore, when trying to decide the best synonym, it is important to think of the context (the other words in the sentence or surrounding sentence) in order for you to choose a synonym with the correct meaning for the situation. For example, consider the following uses of the word "quiet."

1) The professor told the students to be quiet during the exam.

In this sentence, it means "silent."

2) She usually has a quiet cup of tea in the afternoon.

In this sentence, it means "relaxed."

3) The criminal went quiet about the burglary to the police

In this sentence, it means "tight-lipped," i.e. that he is trying to hide something.

4) The cashier took money out of the register in quiet.

In this sentence, it means "in secret."

Denotative and Connotative Meanings

Another reason that two words with the same meaning cannot always be used as synonyms is that words have different connotations – nuances or feelings (see Chapter A2.1 for more details). Therefore, despite having essentially the same meaning, different synonyms are used to fit the context (purpose and situation) of the writing. For example, take the words "group," "club," "clique" and "faction." All of these words have virtually the same dictionary (denotative) meaning, yet they have very different emotional (connotative) meanings. The word "group" is neutral, with no particular negative or positive emotions connected to the meaning. However, "club" has a more positive feeling, referring to a group of people who are friendly and share similar interests. In contrast, "clique" is used negatively because, while "clique" still means "group," it refers to a group with narrow, unfriendly and selfish interests. Finally, when a "clique" becomes a "faction," it can take on an even more negative feeling, depending on the context. "Faction" is sometimes negative, often used to describe a group of people that aggressively advances its own interests.

Collocations

Finally, a synonym of another word sometimes cannot be used in certain situations due to the word being part of a collocation – words that must appear together (see Chapter A2.4 for more details). For example, the word "commit" can take a meaning such as "to do," but only in collocations that indicate a crime. Therefore, you can say "commit a crime" or "commit fraud," but never "commit a sport" or "commit a part-time job." Similarly, it would be strange to say "do a crime" or "do fraud." Chapter A2.4 contains some common collocations that you should know, but for this chapter, be aware that knowing collocations can help you decide whether or not a synonym is appropriate.

Example of Synonym Vocabulary in Use

This following passage is adapted from George Orwell's 1945 novella *Animal Farm*. Read the passage and answer the synonym vocabulary questions.

Original Passage

…Remember always your duty of enmity towards Man and all his ways. Moreover, remember that in fighting against Man, we must not come to resemble him. Even when you have conquered him, do not adopt his vices. No animal must ever live in a house, or sleep in a bed, or wear clothes, or drink alcohol, or smoke tobacco, or touch money, or engage in trade. All the habits of Man are evil... Above all, no animal must ever tyrannize over his own kind…Old Major cleared his throat and began to sing. As he had said, his voice was hoarse, but he sang well enough, and it was a stirring tune. The words ran: 'Beasts of England, beasts of Ireland…' The singing of this song threw the animals into the wildest excitement…

1) In the passage, the word "vices" has the closest meaning to:
   (A) households
   (B) bad habits
   (C) victories
   (D) fights

2) In the passage, the word "tyrannize" has the closest meaning to:
   (A) bullying
   (B) controller
   (C) oppress
   (D) imitation

3) In the passage, the word "stirring" has the closest meaning to:
   (A) uplifting
   (B) pleading
   (C) angering
   (D) mixing

The answer to question 1 is "B." This is an example of how you can choose the correct synonym from an illustrative phrase, in this case, the list of bad habits. The answer to question 2 is "C." The suffix "-ize" makes this word a present tense verb, and only "C" is a verb. This is an example of using word parts and word families to get the correct synonym. The answer to question 3 is "A." Although "to stir" can mean "to mix," "stirring" can also mean "inspiring," and in this context "to mix" does not make sense. This is an example of using context to choose the correct synonym.

A1.3 Skimming and Scanning

Skimming is a technique that enables readers to get the main idea of a long text quickly and efficiently. Scanning involves readers swiftly finding specific keywords and phrases and in order to identify and understand key information in the surrounding text. Skimming and scanning is important for Tohoku University students because doing background reading for research projects, and many upper-division (3rd and 4th year) and graduate courses requires students to get a lot of important information from written texts in a short time. Additionally, skimming and scanning can be very useful when taking standardized English tests.

What to Know about Skimming and Scanning

Skimming text involves rapidly moving the eyes over the pages and paying close attention to any prominent features, such as tables, charts, headings, numbered lists, bold text, italic text, parenthetical text, nouns, dates, names and numbers. It is also important to read the first and last sentences of each paragraph. By doing so, the reader will be able to determine the general topic of the piece of writing without having to read every word. While skimming, the reader must take notes, identify keywords and highlight any potentially important information.

Scanning assumes the reader is looking for facts, information, keywords or answers to particular questions. When scanning, readers should physically point out and highlight (circle, underline, notate) keywords that they have already established through skimming or those that they got from any questions, worksheets or additional materials already assigned. While scanning, the reader usually can ignore all other words until coming across a keyword. At this point, the reader must stop and carefully read the text surrounding the keyword or phrase as thoroughly as possible. When possible, readers should look up unknown words and highlight sentences that contain information related to the keywords. This should be done carefully and attentively, as it is very easy to overlook important sentences in dense text.

The idea of not reading every word in a text may make some readers feel uncomfortable at first—especially during examinations. The key to mastering the techniques of skimming and scanning is to practice regularly. In time, both reading speed and comprehension will significantly improve.

Example of Skimming and Scanning in Use

Below is a reading passage with several comprehension questions similar to a standardized English test. Practice by doing the following:

1. Skim the following reading passage as described above, identifying keywords and phrases.
2. Read the comprehension questions thoroughly and highlight keywords and phrases.
3. Scan the passage as described above, looking for keywords and phrases found in #2 above.
4. Answer the comprehension questions.

<u>Reading Passage</u>

The Transition Period

In the 18th century, before close contact with the conquering Europeans, there were seven tribes of Sioux-Nation Indians in North America, each of which boasted notable men at their helm. Chiefs such as Redwing, Little Six, Hump and Conquering Bear famously led their respective tribes. However, these chiefs were the last of an old, earlier type of Indian chief. During the mid-19th century – in a time known as the transition period – a coterie of new leaders emerged. They were products of the changed conditions brought about by the new realities of having to coexist with the colonists. This distinction must be borne in mind – the early chiefs were merely spokespersons, advisors and elders for and to their tribe. They possessed no absolute authority over their people.

Red Cloud

However, those who headed their tribes once the transition period began can be described as true rulers, leaders and politicians. Chief Red Cloud was one such transition period chief. He was born in 1822 near the forks of the Platte River in what is now the US State of Nebraska. He was one of nine children whose father, an able and respected warrior, reared his son under the old Spartan regime. The young Red Cloud was a fine equestrian, able to swim strongly across rivers, had a respectful personality and unquestionable courage. Yet, he was invariably gentle and courteous to everyone in his daily life. This last trait, together with a singularly musical and agreeable voice, has always been his most recognized characteristic.

Youth

When he was about six years old, his father gave him a spirited colt. With the gift, he said to him: "My son, when you are able to sit quietly upon the back of this horse without saddle or bridle, I shall be glad, for the boy who can tame a wild creature and learn to use it will, as a grown man, be able to win over and rule men." The little fellow, instead of going his grandfather for advice and help on exactly how to do this – as was the custom of his tribe – began to practice throwing a lariat quietly on his own. In time, he was able to lasso the horse. He was dragged off his feet more than once but learned to hang on, finally managing to picket horses with ease.

In time, the boy was able to ride bareback; he was thrown many times but persisted until he could ride without a lariat, sitting with arms folded and guiding the animal by the movements of his body. From that time on, he broke all his own ponies, and his father's as well. His contemporaries often related how Red Cloud was always successful in the hunt because his horses were so well broken.

Lessons Learned

At age nine, he began to ride along in the buffalo hunts. By twelve, he was permitted to take part in his first buffalo chase. In a watershed incident, as he tried to bag his first buffalo, he found to his great mortification that his arrows had not penetrated the beast more than a few inches. Excited to recklessness, he whipped his horse nearer the fleeing buffalo, and before his father knew what he was doing, he seized one of the protruding arrows and tried to push it in deeper with his hand. The furious animal tossed his massive head sidewise, and the boy and horse were whirled into the air. Fortunately, the boy was thrown on the farther side of his pony, which received the full force of the attack. The thundering hoofs of the stampeding herd soon passed him by, but the wounded and maddened buffalo refused to move, snorting angrily at the lad. Some critical moments passed before Red Cloud's father succeeded in attracting the animal's attention away so that the boy could spring to his feet and run to safety.

Legacy

This experience at such a young age taught Red Cloud a meaningful lesson about respecting adversaries. This incident served him very well for he grew up to become one of the most effective, revered and respected Indian chiefs, leaders, warriors, and diplomats in American history.

(Adapted from Charles Eastman, *Indian Heroes and Great Chieftains* (1918))

Below are some examples from the passage of potential skimmed keywords and phrases (underlined) that may help you understand the overall passage.

In the 18th century, before close contact with the conquering Europeans, there were seven tribes of Sioux-Nation Indians in North America, each of which boasted notable men at their helm. This distinction must be borne in mind – the early chiefs were merely spokespersons, advisors and elders for their tribe and possessed no real authority over their people.

However, those who headed their tribes once the <u>transition period</u> began can be described as true rulers, leaders and politicians.

This last <u>trait</u>, together with a singularly musical and agreeable voice, has always been his <u>most recognized</u> characteristic.

When he was about six years old, his father gave him a <u>spirited colt.</u>

He was dragged off his feet more than once but learned to hang on, finally managing to <u>picket horses</u> with ease.

In time, the boy was able to ride bareback; he was thrown many times but <u>persisted</u> until he could ride without even a lariat, sitting with arms folded and guiding the animal by the movements of his body.

His contemporaries often related how Red Cloud was always successful in the hunt because his horses were <u>so well broken</u>.

At age nine, he began to <u>take part in</u> buffalo hunts.

Some <u>critical moments</u> passed before Red Cloud's father succeeded in attracting the animal's attention so that the boy could spring to his feet and run to safety.

This experience at such a young age taught him a meaningful lesson about <u>respect for adversaries</u>.

<u>This lesson</u> served him very well as he grew up to become one of the most effective, revered and respected Indian chiefs, leaders, warriors, and diplomats in American history.

Note the potential keywords and phrases in the comprehension questions. Examples of some potential keywords and phrases are <u>underlined.</u>

1) What is this passage mainly about?
    (A) Sioux Indian Chiefs
    (B) Red Cloud's training as a <u>youth</u>
    (C) Indian Buffalo hunts
    (D) Red Cloud's horse-riding abilities

2) In paragraph one, the word "<u>coterie</u>" can best be replaced by
    (A) courage
    (B) corsage
    (C) group
    (D) colonial

3) In paragraph five, the phrase "<u>watershed incident</u>" is closest in meaning to
    (A) marine episode
    (B) hydro event
    (C) accident
    (D) defining moment

4) What <u>trait</u> is Red Cloud most recognized for?
    (A) courteousness
    (B) bravery
    (C) agreeable voice
    (D) recklessness

5) What lesson did Red Cloud learn at a young age that enabled him to grow up to become one of the most <u>revered</u> leaders in American history?
    (A) riding a spirited colt
    (B) throwing a lariat
    (C) buffalo hunting
    (D) having esteem for his opponents

Scan the passage as described above, looking for keywords and phrases found in #2. Highlight the keywords and phrases selected from both the passage and the comprehension questions and then read the text surrounding the keywords carefully. Below are examples of some potential scanned keywords and phrases from both the text and the comprehension questions:

buffalo hunts	colt	trait
coterie	watershed incident	adversaries
gentle	courteous	learned
American history	recklessness	so well broken
mortification	revered leader	persisted
distinction	Red Cloud	youth

The answer to question 1 is "B." By skimming and scanning, it is clear the passage is about Red Cloud's youth. The answer to question 2 is "C." It is clear the sentences surrounding the word "coterie" refer to "new leaders." Leaders are people and people are classified into "groups." The answer to question 3 is "D." The sentences surrounding the phrase "watershed incident" refer to an event. In this case, the event caused Red Cloud to learn, change, grow up and *define* him as a man. The answer to question 4 is "A" The sentences surrounding the word "trait" list several of his characteristics. "This last trait" refers to his courtesy as being the "most recognized." The answer to question 5 is "D." Red Cloud learned all these lessons. However, scanning around the word "revered" reveals that it was learning "respect for his adversaries" that enabled him to become "revered."

A1.4 Summarizing and Paraphrasing

Paraphrasing is the act of restating what is read or heard in your own words, without necessarily shortening the original text. A well-written paraphrase should (1) use sentence structures that differ from those in the original, (2) retain all the major information, and (3) avoid reusing vocabulary and phrases used in the original. Summarizing, on the other hand, is the act of rewriting text that is either read or heard to produce a condensed version of the original. However, it does not only involve shortening the text. In fact, a good summary should (1) include all of the major points and relevant details of the text, (2) contain all of the author's main ideas, and (3) eliminate only minor details. Summarizing and paraphrasing are necessary when writing about or presenting other people's work.

What to Know about Summarizing and Paraphrasing

Summaries and paraphrases must be written in the writer's own words, unless using quotations and references properly (see Chapter C1.2). Presenting the original writer's exact words as one's own work is called plagiarism, which is a serious offense. Listed below are some guidelines that are needed to master summarizing and paraphrasing to avoid plagiarizing someone else's work.

Paraphrasing
Begin by changing the structure of the original passages and sentences. Changing parts of speech, tense, and voice and using reduction are effective ways to do this. To change the part of speech of a word, use suffixes (see Chapter A1.1) and other word parts (see Chapter A1.2).

> Original: Students are generally excited at the prospect of receiving scholarships.
> Paraphrase: In general, students were excited by prospective scholarships.

Notice that "generally" (adverb) was changed to the phrase "in general," and "prospect" (noun) was changed to "prospective" (adjective). The verb was changed to the past tense; however, in this case, this change did not significantly alter the meaning of the sentence. Another way to paraphrase is to change the writing from passive to active voice or vice versa, as in the example below.

> Original: Students are generally excited by the prospect of receiving scholarships.
> Paraphrase: The prospect of receiving scholarships generally excites students.

This paraphrase switched the subject and object positions of the original and used the third-person singular form of the verb "to excite" rather than the past tense. Finally, paraphrasing can be accomplished by reduction – for example, changing a clause to a phrase. A clause is a group of words consisting of a subject and the finite form of a verb and might or might not be a sentence, whereas a phrase cannot stand alone as a sentence.

Original: Students who love to read books are excited by scholarships.
Paraphrase: Book-loving students are excited by scholarships.

In the example above, "who love to read books" is a clause that contains a subject, verb, and object and can stand alone as the sentence, "Students love to read books." However, in the paraphrase, the clause is reduced to the phrase "book-loving students," which cannot be a sentence, though it has the same meaning as "Students who love to read books." Reduction can also be used to avoid repetition of words. For example, "prospective scholarships" indicates the meaning of "scholarships that students might receive," so it is not necessary to repeat the word "receive" when changing the word "prospect" to "prospective." Take note, however, that important information must not be omitted when reducing.

Original: Students who receive exceptional marks throughout the semester have
                     the chance to receive up to $10,000 in scholarships.
Good Paraphrase: There is a chance for students who maintain good grades all semester
                     to receive scholarships of up to $10,000.
Bad Paraphrase: Good students will receive $10,000 in scholarships.

The good paraphrase changes the original sentence's structure and reduces the clause "who receive exceptional marks all semester" while retaining its meaning. The bad paraphrase changes the meaning of the original sentence by omitting important information. For example, "good students" does not necessarily mean students who receive "exceptional marks all semester." It could simply mean well-behaved or highly motivated students. Furthermore, the "chance to receive" has been reduced to "will receive." This is not accurate, because the original statement indicates that even students "who receive exceptional marks throughout the semester" may not, in fact, receive a scholarship.

When paraphrasing, use synonyms to replace the words in the original text (see Chapter A1.2). Obviously, proper nouns and specialized technical terms do not have synonyms, but English has a rich variety of words with similar or identical meanings that native speakers use interchangeably to avoid repetition.

Original:	Albert Einstein is *famous* for his *revolutionary* theories of physics, which *altered* how *we think about* the universe.
Paraphrase:	Albert Einstein is *renowned* for his *novel* theories of physics, which *transformed our understanding* of the universe.

Summarizing

To summarize, first identify both the main idea of the text and the important supporting information. Then write a shortened version of the original text that includes only these points and information. Be sure to write it in your own words using tips from the paraphrasing section.

1. Take Notes While Reading the Passage

When taking notes, organize them according to main points and supporting details, as discussed in Chapter B1.1.

2. Use the Notes While Writing the Summary

When writing the summary, use only your notes – do not rely on the original text. Include only the main ideas and supporting details. Omit minor details, examples, and personal opinions.

3. Check the Summary

After summarizing, compare your summary with the original passage and make sure that it is (1) written in your own words, (2) grammatically correct and (3) factually correct and accurate with respect to important information such as names, places, data, and technical terms.

Example of Summarizing and Paraphrasing in Use

Below is a reading passage followed by a short summary with paraphrases.

Original Article

Although there have been many tragic periods throughout European history, the Late Middle Ages is considered the most devastating. In fact, this era, typically defined as extending from 1250 to 1500, is often referred to as part of the Dark Ages. Its end ushered in a much brighter period for Europe, known as the Renaissance. While the Late Middle Ages saw many misfortunes, historians have identified the three most noteworthy calamities of the period as a devastating famine, a deadly plague, and an extended war.

Famines were common throughout much of the Late Middle Ages. However, a particularly prominent food shortage was the Great Famine of 1315–1317. In the spring of 1315, bad weather led to massive crop failures. To make matters worse, the crop failures coincided with a number of animal diseases that killed 80% of the livestock used for food. The resulting famine lasted for over two years. During that time, it is estimated that between 10% and 20% of people living in urban areas starved to death. Those that remained were forced to turn to begging, crime, and even cannibalism to survive.

However, an even darker period in European history came about 30 years later, when the continent was overcome with the bubonic plague, also known as the Black Death. Over a four-year period, this lethal pandemic caused somewhere between 25 and 200 million deaths. In addition, the pestilence affected the economies of Europe in profound ways by shrinking the labor force, increasing wages, and causing unprecedented mobility among the peasant class.

The longest military conflict in European history also occurred during the Late Middle Ages. Although it is known as the Hundred Years' War, the conflict actually lasted 116 years, from 1337 to 1453, and took the lives of two to three million people. The entire war actually consisted of three Anglo-Franco conflicts lasting 23 years, 20 years, and 38 years, respectively. The hostilities were punctuated by two truces, one lasting nine years and the other 26. The cause of the war was the gradual buildup of tensions regarding which branch of the various French and English monarchies should take control of the male line of the Capetian dynasty and thereby assume the French throne. In the end, the House of Valois – one of the French monarchies – was victorious.

Summary with Paraphrases

Three significant deadly catastrophes occurred in Europe during the Late Middle Ages (1250–1500): widespread starvation, a lethal epidemic, and unrelenting fighting. Mass starvation was caused by bad weather, which led to agricultural failures and lethal cattle diseases from 1315 to 1317. This killed much of the population and drove others to begging, crime, and even cannibalism. The most notable epidemic was the Black Death, which peaked between 1347 and 1351 and killed between 25 and 200 million people, while also severely affecting the economies of Europe. Lastly, the predominant war of the period was the so-called Hundred Years' War, which was actually three conflicts that raged between 1337 and 1453. The war began as a result of the long-standing animosity between the various royal houses of France and England regarding the male lineage of the Capetian dynasty, which held the rights to the French throne.

English B1

Academic Listening and Speaking

Objective 1: Acquire the ability to take notes

B1.1 Note-Taking While Listening
B1.2 Orally Summarizing from Notes

Objective 2: Acquire the ability to use common spoken academic expressions

B1.3 Interrogatives and Giving Opinions
B1.4 Phrasal Verbs and Idiomatic Expressions

B1.1 Note-Taking While Listening

Note-taking is critical in academic settings. Though it can also help readers to organize and remember important information later, it is especially important when listening to lectures. This is because students will need to study the presented information later, but they will only hear it once. Note-taking also helps listeners to be more attentive, because it makes them responsible for identifying key information and organizing it clearly so that they can review it later. This skill will, therefore, be useful for students at Tohoku University when conducting research, listening to lectures, and participating in laboratory activities.

What to Know about Note-Taking While Listening

Listening to a lecture or long talk is different from listening to or participating in a conversation or discussion because lectures and talks are structured and contain specific information that must be remembered later for exams, essays, or reports. While there are several different ways to take notes, all styles require listening for signal words and phrases, organizing the notes appropriately, and writing quickly.

Identifying Information via Signal Words and Phrases
When a speaker gives a lecture or long talk in English, they will use signal words and phrases, as well as repetition and voice inflection (see Chapter C2.2), to give clues as to what information is important and what type of information it is. Memorize the list of common signal words and phrases in the chart below, and when they appear, make sure to listen to the surrounding information and identify it correctly. The words in parentheses are not necessary, but often occur together with the other words.

Introducing Topics			
Today… (indicates topic)	(what) we are / were discussing is…	I'm gonna / I want to talk about…	What is…?
Introducing or Changing Main Ideas			
Let's look at…	First, second, third…/ another <point> / next…	Let's move on…	Important / main / major / critical / key
I'd like to mention…	You should note (that)…	The role of…	

Giving Facts and Numbers			
You might want to / ought to know (that)…	As you can see…	Keep in mind (that)…	The relationship/ difference between…
In the sense that…	Well…	In fact…	Basically…
Giving Explanations			
(so) You can see (that) …(from)…	You see…	The thing is…	(see) what I'm saying is…
If you think about it…	In other words…	In this respect…	But first…/ however / though
Giving Reasons and Results			
It turns out (that)…	In order to…	The reason why / for…	In turn…
…leads to…			
Giving Examples			
Take <example>	If you look at <example>	When you look at…	Including / like /…and so forth
For example / an example of…	For instance…		
Defining Terms			
…referred to as…	which is (called)…	…(also) known as…	According to …

Organizing Information

When taking notes, it is important to show how different pieces of information relate to one another. As indicated by the chart in the previous section, there are different types of information, but they can be broadly classified into two categories: main points and supporting details. In general, it is a good idea to write a main idea on a single line, and then write all of the related supporting details underneath. While a speaker usually only has one large topic, they often have several main points about the topic. Each of these main points is then usually supported by several details. There are different types of details, but they can be categorized as facts and numbers, term definitions, reasons, results, explanations, and examples. These are similar to the supporting information that is often given in writing, as discussed in Chapter A2.3. However, be aware that there are some words and phrases that are more common in spoken English than in written English (compare the chart in the previous section to the one in Chapter A2.3).

Writing Quickly

When taking notes about a text, there is no need to write quickly. However, when taking notes about a lecture, listeners cannot write at their own pace because the speaker will continue to talk, and the listener will need to catch the new information as well. Here are some tips to write quickly and efficiently when taking notes.

1. Use abbreviations and symbols instead of words when you can.

Abbreviations are shortened forms of words, and some symbols are often used in place of words. Some abbreviations are famous (e.g., World Health Organization → WHO, United States of America → USA, etc.), but personalized abbreviations can be used as well if the note taker can understand them later (e.g., "international" → "int'l," "government" → "gov't," etc.). Similarly, some symbols are well known (e.g., and → &), but others are available (e.g. and → +), and the ones that are easiest for the note-taker to write and recognize should be used. Below is a list of some common abbreviations and symbols. Consider using some of these when taking notes.

with, without	w/, w/o	**about/regarding**	re.
because	b/c	**number**	#
chapter	ch.	**and**	&, +
for example	e.g.	**is / equals**	=
specifically	i.e.	**at**	@

2. Write phrases, not full sentences

When taking notes while listening, there will probably not be enough time to write full sentences. Consider reducing important information to simple phrases. For example, instead of writing "World War II took place between 1939 and 1945 among America, Britain, France, Soviets, Germany, Italy, Japan," try writing something like "WWII: 1939–1945 among US, GB, FR, USSR, DE, IT, JPN."

3. Paraphrase

To paraphrase is to re-write a speaker or writer's words in your own words. Though Chapter A1.4 provides more detail about paraphrasing in writing, paraphrasing should mostly be done during note-taking while listening in order to shorten what a speaker is saying. It is not necessary for the listener to write exactly what a speaker has said, as long as the basic information is correct. So, remove any unnecessary words from the speaker's remarks, and write in a way that is true to the lecture or talk but is short and easy to understand. For example, instead of writing "So anyway, it is important to know that Vincent van Gogh was never a commercially successful painter because his work didn't sell well until after his death," the following could be used when note-taking: "van Gogh didn't make money painting; his art sold better after he died."

Other Tips for Note-Taking While Listening

In general, it is also a good idea to prepare before listening as much as possible. For lectures and talks, this means doing any assigned reading or research before listening, and for standardized tests, this means checking the questions before listening to guess what information will be important to catch. If there are any prepared materials, for example, handouts or test questions that are available before listening, try to make predictions about what will be said based on what is known about the topic or related words. Finally, it is also a good idea to leave blank space when taking notes. If a listener misses important information while listening to a lecture, they can ask the speaker or their classmates to help them fill in the missing information later.

Example of Note-Taking While Listening in Use

Try listening to the lecture linked in the QR code at the end. Then, look at the text of the lecture below and the sample notes taken about this topic. Notice how the signal words and phrases, highlighted in **bold**, clearly mark the important information (underlined). Recognize that the notes are well organized. It is also clear what the main points are and which supporting details are attached to which main points. Finally, also notice that the notes make good use of abbreviations, symbols, phrases, and paraphrasing.

Example lecture text

Okay, um, so **today we are going to talk about** what plants do for the ecosystem, which is academically **referred to as** "ecological services." These services are how plants support other members of the ecosystem, specifically animals. In this lesson, I'm going to outline how several of these "ecological services" work. **The first** of these key services is **known as** the carbon-oxygen cycle. The basis of this cycle is photosynthesis, **which is** when a plant absorbs carbon dioxide from the atmosphere and water from the ground to produce oxygen and glucose for plant growth. We talked about this a little bit last class, but I, I really want to mention here that this process is so important because when animals breathe, they convert oxygen into carbon dioxide, so **in fact**, they need plants to create oxygen for their survival. So, remember to thank a plant for your oxygen today. Furthermore, when plants die, they decompose, and the carbon returns to the soil so that it can be utilized by other plants and animals. Now, let's uh…, **let's move on** to **talk about** how plants also provide energy for the entire ecosystem. **Keep in mind that** plants get the energy needed for photosynthesis directly from the sun. If you, um, if you did your homework, you should know that already. **If you think about it,** animals cannot create energy themselves, so they have to eat these plants or other animals for energy. Maybe you think that carnivores don't need plants, but **the thing is**, <u>even if an animal does not eat plants directly, it eats animals that do</u>, so **in other words**, <u>all animals rely on plants for energy</u>…

Example of notes based on the above lecture)

What plants do for the ecosystem
I. Ecological services
→ support ecosystem members (i.e. animals)

    1. Carbon-oxygen cycle
    → photosynthesis = absorb CO_2 & water → oxygen & glucose
    → animals need plants b/c their breathing = oxygen → CO_2
    → plant death = carbon returns to soil for others' use

    2. Provide Energy
    → plants get energy from sun
    → animals cannot get energy from sun
    → animals rely on plants b/c they eat plants or other animals

B1.2 Orally Summarizing from Notes

Orally summarizing from notes is the process of looking at notes previously taken from a reading, lecture, talk or recording, determining the important information, and communicating it verbally. This skill is important for Tohoku University students, as they will often need to check the accuracy of their notes from their reading assignments, lectures, and laboratory work and discuss them with other students and teachers. In addition, students in English language learning environments will be expected to be able to give spoken summaries of their notes.

What to Know about Orally Summarizing from Notes

To successfully summarize notes orally, there are three steps: choosing both primary information and secondary evidence, organizing the information clearly, and verbally communicating the information.

Choosing the Important Information

Orally summarizing is not repeating exactly what has been read or heard but rather putting it into paraphrase form (see Chapter A1.4). It is important, however, to list all of the main topics and points and elaborate (give supporting details) on each. To elaborate, one should highlight details from the source material such as examples, descriptions, reasons, and explanations.

Organizing the Information Clearly

To organize information clearly, students should consider making a basic outline of their notes, which can make it easier to produce a summary. The outline itself does not need to be detailed – it should simply be used as a reference for what must be said and in what order. Once the information has been organized into an outline, it becomes much easier to verbally summarize by introducing the topic's main points, elaborating on the details, and using transition vocabulary to give examples. An example outline is provided below.

Topic – Points – Supporting Information

I. TOPIC
Sea mammals

II. MAIN POINT:
Similarity with land mammals

III. SUPPORTING INFORMATION

    A. *Oxygen intake*

      1. *Surface breathing*

        a. *Manatees*

    B. *Nourishing young*

      1. *Milk*

        a. *Dolphins*

    C. *Hair follicles*

      1. *Hair-like structures*

      a. *Sea otters*

Verbally Communicating the Information

The chart below provides phrases that can be used to verbally communicate using the written outline. To effectively communicate notes orally, memorize the phrases in the chart below and from Chapter B1.1 (Note Taking while Listening), as well as other useful phrases found in Chapters A1.2 and A1.4 (Synonym Vocabulary, and Summarizing and Paraphrasing).

Introducing a Main Point	Elaborating on Points	Transitioning
The first (second/third) point brought up by the speaker/author is…	One (another) reason the speaker/author thinks so is that…	This brings up another major point/reason/issue…
One (another) reason why the speaker/author thinks so is…	One (another) example that shows this is…	Moving on to the next (second/third) point/issue…
One (another) important issue the speaker/author talks about is…	Also/furthermore/in addition, the speaker/author mentions that…	However, the speaker/author also has another important issue/point...
One (another) major topic is…	Specifically, the speaker/author says that…	For example, the speaker/author points out that…

Though pronunciation and intonation (see Chapter B2.3) are important when speaking, the key skill for orally summarizing your notes is clear communication of ideas. Specifically, complete sentences and proper transition vocabulary must be used. Be especially careful not to leave out the sentence's subject or premise (main idea), as this is a common mistake among Japanese learners of English. Also, be aware that overuse of the word "so" can cause students to accidentally create a logical connection between two sentences that does not exist, which can confuse listeners. Examples of this are shown below:

	Mistake	**Corrected**
Missing subject or premise	Talks about climate change.	→ The passage talks about climate change.
	Changes in DNA by virus.	→ Viruses cause changes in DNA.
Unrelated information / improperly connected information	Many people are worried… so global warming is getting serious.	→ Many people are worried because global warming is getting serious.
	Virus DNA changes… so scientists study the DNA of some plants.	→ Studying the DNA of some plants helps scientists understand how virus DNA can change.
	Recycling is important… so it is damaging the Earth.	→ Recycling is important… because not doing it is damaging the Earth.

Example of Orally Summarizing from Notes in Use

Look at some sample notes from Chapter B1.1. Below is an example of an oral summary from these notes. Words and phrases introduced in this chapter are in bold. A QR code is also provided at the end of the chapter that links to a recording of this summary.

Outline for Oral Summary
I. TOPIC
What plants do for the ecosystem: Ecological services

II. MAIN POINT 1:
Carbon-oxygen cycle

III. SUPPORTING INFORMATION
    A. ***Photosynthesis***
      1. *Absorb CO_2 & water*
      2. *Makes oxygen & glucose*
    B. ***Animals need plants***
      1. *They breathe oxygen*
      2. *Make CO_2*
    C. ***Plant death***
      1. *Gives carbon back to soil for others*

IV. MAIN POINT 2:
Provide Energy

V. SUPPORTING INFORMATION

A. *Plants get energy from the sun*

1. *Through photosynthesis*
2. *Animals cannot*

B. *Animals need plants*

1. *They have to eat plants or animals for energy*

Example Oral Summary

The **speaker talked about** how plants support the ecosystem through "ecological services." The **first point he introduced** was one of these services, **specifically** the carbon-oxygen cycle. **The key feature** of this cycle is photosynthesis. **The speaker mentioned** that plants use carbon dioxide and water and turn it into oxygen and glucose. **In addition, he mentioned** that animals need plants to do this because they breathe oxygen and make carbon dioxide. **He also pointed out** that when plants die, they give carbon back to the soil so that others can use it. **Moving on, the other ecological service is** providing energy. **The speaker says** that plants get energy from the sun through photosynthesis, and that animals cannot. **Specifically, he says** that animals need plants for their energy because they have to eat plants or other animals for energy instead.

Compare this oral summary to the original lecture in Chapter B1.1. It is somewhat shorter than the original, but uses some of the key vocabulary (i.e. "ecosystem," "ecological," "photosynthesis"). Some of the words used in the summary have been replaced with phrasal verbs, making the summary simpler and more like spoken English (see Chapter B1.4) (i.e. absorb – take in; release – let out). Notice, however, that the sentences, though simpler, still have clear subjects and use clear transition vocabulary.

B1.3 Interrogatives and Giving Opinions

"Interrogative" is an English grammatical term referring to a word or sentence used to ask a question. Forming grammatically correct questions is a fundamental skill in English that students will need when requesting information. Furthermore, when answering questions, students will often be required to give their opinion and defend their position with details and evidence. Therefore, mastering these skills is essential for participating in a wide variety of academic activities at Tohoku University, such as discussions, research activities, group work, and classes.

What to Know about Interrogatives and Giving Opinions

Word order is very important when forming questions. Using incorrect word order or the wrong question word can lead the listener to misunderstand the question. Similarly, answering a question correctly requires that the listener has understood what is being asked. Therefore, the first step to mastering interrogatives is to learn the types of questions and the word order related to each type.

Closed Questions

Closed questions are those that can be answered simply with "yes" or "no" and are created using the inversion method. This means that "be" verbs, modal verbs (see Chapter A2.2) and helping verbs ("be," "do," and "have") should be moved before the subject. For other verbs, the verb "do" should be placed at the beginning of the sentence.

> He is a university student. → Is he a university student? ("is" moves before "he")
> She {does} skis. → Does she ski? ("does" moves before "she")

Open Questions

Another way to ask a question is by using interrogative words, or wh-question words. When a wh-question word is used, the reply requires more detail than just a simple "yes" or "no." Therefore, the responder has a range of replies from which to choose. These questions are called "open questions." Below is a list of the wh-question words and the expected responses.

Wh-Question Word	Expected Response
who	a person as the subject or object of a verb
whom	a person as the indirect object of the preposition "to," "with," "for," or "by"
whose	a person as possessor

which	an object, idea or action selected from several possible options
what	a specific object, idea or action
when	a general time or time period
where	a location
why	a reason
how	a manner, method or technique

Open questions are typically formed by first applying the inversion method and then putting the wh-question word at the beginning of the sentence. However, in certain cases, the wh-question word has a special function, in which case the word order will change, as detailed below.

Wh-Question Words as Determiners
Wh-question words used as determiners ("what," "which," and "whose") are placed before a noun to clarify or determine the noun. When forming an interrogative with a wh-question word as a determiner, the noun being modified by the wh-question word must be moved to the beginning of the sentence and placed directly after the wh-question word. See the examples and common mistakes below.

E.g. Questions about **nouns**

    What sport do you like?   **What instrument** can you play?

    ~~What do you like sports?~~   ~~What can you play an instrument?~~

E.g. Questions about the pronouns "one" or "ones"

    Which one did you see?   **Which ones** did you buy?

    ~~Which did you see one?~~   ~~Which bought you ones?~~

E.g. Questions about choice (sometimes used with "of" if plural)

    Which sushi shall we eat first?   **Which of these cars** can we rent?

    ~~Which shall we eat first sushi?~~   ~~Which can we rent of these cars?~~

E.g. Questions about a possessor

    Whose novels does he like?   **Whose bicycle** was stolen?

    ~~Whose does he like novels?~~   ~~Who was stolen their bicycle?~~

Wh-Question Words as Adverbs
Wh-question words used as adverbs refer to times, locations, methods, purposes, or reasons. When forming an interrogative with a wh-question word as an adverb, the wh-question word should be placed at the beginning of the sentence after using the inversion method. If the adverb is modifying a specific adjective, adverb, or phrase, that word must be moved to the beginning

of the sentence and placed directly after the wh-question word. See the examples and common mistakes below.

When – Questions about **times**
    When will you leave?
    ~~Will you leave when?~~

Where – Questions about **places**
    Where do your parents live?
    ~~Do your parents live where?~~

How – Questions about **methods**

    How did you get to school?
    ~~How you get to school?~~

Why – Questions about **reasons**
    Why are you driving so fast?
    ~~Why you are driving so fast?~~

How old – Questions about **ages**
(of anything)
    How old is that house?
    ~~How many years is that house old?~~

How + adjective – Questions about **degree**
    How tall is he?
    ~~How much tall is he?~~

Why – Questions about **purposes**
    Why are you doing that?
    ~~Why you are doing that?~~

How come – (same as "why")
    How come you're studying?
    ~~How do you come studying?~~

How much/many – Questions about **quantity**
    How much rice can you eat?
    ~~How many rice can you eat?~~

How far – Questions about **distances**
    How far is it from your house to here?
    ~~How is it distance from your house?~~

How + adverb – about **timing/rating/etc.**

    How soon can you arrive? (timing)
    ~~How many quickly can you get here?~~
    How well can you ski? (rating)
    ~~How good do you skiing?~~

Note: "Many" is used for countable nouns, and "much" is used for non-countable nouns.

Wh-Question Words as Pronouns

Wh-question words used as pronouns ("who," "which," "whose," "whom," and "what") refer to a noun that they replace in a statement. When forming an interrogative with a wh-question word as a pronoun, the wh-question word should be placed at the beginning of the sentence after using the inversion method, and the word that the pronoun is replacing should be removed from the sentence.

Who should we hire? – We should hire <u>Ken</u>.

Which is the season you enjoy most? – The season I enjoy most is <u>winter</u>.

Whose blue bicycle is this? – This is <u>John's</u> blue bicycle.

<u>With **whom**</u> do you usually eat lunch? – I usually eat lunch <u>with Sarah</u>.

Note: Be careful not to confuse "whose" (asks about the possessor) and "who's" (the contracted version of "who is"). These words are pronounced the same but are used differently. E.g. **Whose** is that? – *It's <u>Ken's</u>*. **Who's** that? *It is <u>Ken</u>*.

Note: The pronoun "whom" is used as the indirect object, after the prepositions "to," "with," "for," and "by." When forming questions with "whom," the preposition should also be brought to the front of the sentence. However, in colloquial English, "who" is often used instead of "whom," and the preposition is left at the end of the sentence. E.g. (proper English) With whom are you talking? (colloquial English) Who are you talking to?

Tag Questions

Tag questions (also called "tags") are another way of turning statements into closed questions, which is usually done to ask for confirmation. They are formed by adding a comma to the end of the sentence, then repeating the auxiliary or modal verb, changing it to negative or positive, and then giving the subject as a pronoun. If the sentence does not contain an auxiliary or modal verb, the verb "do" should be used as the auxiliary. For positive statements, a negative tag must be used, and for negative statements, a positive tag is needed. Furthermore, negative tag questions require that the verb be in the negative contracted form. See the examples and common mistakes below.

Emiko is an excellent student, isn't she? (positive statement + negative tag)

You play soccer, don't you? (positive statement + negative tag)

It won't rain tonight, will it? (negative statement + positive tag)

You've never been to the UK, have you? (negative statement + positive tag)

~~Emiko is an excellent student, is she?~~ (positive statements need negative tags)

~~You don't play soccer, isn't it?~~ (wrong verb and wrong pronoun in the tag)

Rhetorical Questions

Rhetorical questions are those that the speaker does not expect an answer to. Grammatically, they are usually formed in the same manner as other questions, and the listener must use clues about the situation to recognize that they are rhetorical (see Chapter B2.1). However, one style of rhetorical question that has a different grammatical form is the un-inverted question. An un-inverted question is one in which the verb is not moved to the head of the sentence and the wh-question word is not moved to the head of the sentence. However, the wh-question word will still appear at the beginning of the sentence if it would naturally occur there anyway (e.g. when used as the determiner of the subject or as a pronoun that is the subject of the sentence). Un-inverted questions are generally used to express surprise at new information that the speaker has received, and the specific piece of information that surprised them is generally marked with a wh-question word. Here are some examples:

You ate **what**?! (the speaker is surprised about what was eaten, not who ate it)
Who ate it?! (the speaker is surprised about who ate it, not what was eaten)
He looked at **whose** cat?! (the speaker is surprised about the owner of the cat)
You went to school **how**?! (the speaker is surprised by the method of going to school)

Embedded Questions

Embedded questions are interrogatives that are partially hidden inside other questions or statements to make the question more polite (see Chapter B2.2). When creating an embedded question, the main question (i.e. the question that the speaker wants an answer to) must be un-inverted and treated as a relative clause, because the sentence either becomes a statement, or the grammatical function of asking a question is performed by another part of the sentence. See the examples and common mistakes below.

E.g. embedding a question in a statement
    I would like to know <something>   +   Where is the bathroom?
        = I would like to know where the bathroom is.
        ~~I would like to know where is the bathroom.~~

    I wonder <something>   +   Why do you like that?
        = I wonder why you like that.
        ~~I wonder why do you like that.~~

E.g. embedding a question in another question
    Do you know <something>   +   Where is the train station?
        = Do you know where the train station is?
        ~~Do you know where is the train station?~~

    Can you tell me <something>   +   Who is the teacher for this class?
        = Can you tell me who the teacher for this class is?
        ~~Can you tell me who is the teacher for this class?~~

Question–Response

Giving an appropriate response to a question shows that you correctly understood it. Giving an even partially inappropriate response will confuse the asker and make them think that you did not understand the question. Therefore, it is important to understand what kind of information is being requested (see the previous sections) and give an appropriate answer. See the examples and common mistakes below.

How is it going?
　　It's going well.
　　~~I'm going to school now.~~

Which laboratory should we visit tomorrow?
　　Let's go to Dr. Nakamura's laboratory.
　　~~We should visit a laboratory tomorrow.~~

In the first example, "How is it going?" asks about someone's wellbeing or status, so the answer should use an adjective or adverb and describe their situation. It does not ask **what** someone is doing. In the second example, the question asks for a selection from several options, not whether or not a laboratory should be visited.

Knowing the implication (hidden meaning) of a question will also be important in formulating an appropriate response. For example, as mentioned above, rhetorical questions do not request information and therefore generally should not be answered. Though implication will be covered in more depth in Chapter B2.2, for this chapter, it is important to understand that negative questions and positive statements with negative tags typically indicate that the asker thinks the premise is not true, whereas tag questions indicate that the asker thinks the premise is true. Examples of this are given below, with the asker's guess written in (parentheses).

Doesn't she look like her sister? (you think she looks like her sister)
Can't we attend the party too? (you will say we can attend the party too)
You play soccer, don't you? (you play soccer)
You don't play soccer, do you? (you don't play soccer)

When answering questions that contain negative questions, such as those above, it is important to remember that in English, the positive equivalent of the question (without implication) and not the actual question itself should be answered. In other words, answers that begin with "yes" should never be followed by negative statements, and answers that begin with "no" should never be followed by positive statements. When this mistake is made, the asker will become unsure what the answer is, as the response will be contradictory. See the examples and common mistakes below.

Didn't you enjoy Dr. Smith's lecture?

    No, I didn't.

    ~~Yes, I didn't.~~

    Yes, I did.

    ~~No, I did.~~

You don't like pizza, do you?

    No, I don't.

    ~~Yes, I don't~~

    Yes, I do.

    ~~No, I do.~~

Giving Opinions Implicitly and Explicitly

Most questions will require the speaker to give their opinion or an answer based on their beliefs or understanding. While some questions may only require simple answers (e.g. "What is your student number?"), many require a statement of opinion, which is best followed by supporting details. There are several ways that opinions can be given in response to questions, but they can be broadly divided into explicit phrases, which offer opinions very directly, and implicit phrases, which are indirect and therefore politer. Memorize the lists of explicit and implicit phrases below. Notice that the explicit phrases generally use the pronouns "I", "me," or "my," whereas implicit phrases often use pronouns such as "it" or non-person subjects such as "the evidence" to distance the speaker from the opinion.

Explicit Phrases for Giving Opinions

I think/feel/believe...	In my opinion...	It seems to me that...
I hold the view that...	From my point of view...	In my experience...
As far as I'm concerned...	My impression is that...	The way I see it...

Implicit Phrases for Giving Opinions

The evidence suggests that...	It is likely that...	It seems that...
The thing is that...	It makes sense that...	It could be argued that...
It goes without saying...	A case could be made that...	Most people would think...

Supporting Evidence and Details

When giving your opinion, especially in response to a question, it is often best to give more than a simple statement or short answer. Instead, evidence and details should be provided to support the opinion or answer to the question. While there are a number of different types of supporting information that can be provided, when giving an opinion or response to a question, try including reasons, facts and numbers, explanations or examples. The words and phrases that often mark supporting information shown in Chapters B1.1 and B1.2 can be used to do this. Below are some questions to consider when giving supporting evidence and details:

Reasons: why do you think that, or why is that your answer?

Facts and numbers: what background information supports your opinion or answer?

Explanations: what exactly do you mean by your opinion or response? How does your answer address the question?)

Examples: can you give a real-life or imaginary example that shows why you think your opinion or answer is correct?

Example of Giving Opinions and Interrogatives in Use

Look at the example of a question and the four responses shown below. A QR Code linked to a recording of the examples is provided at the end. Notice how the final response is most appropriate because it correctly answers the question and gives a good amount of supporting information for the answer.

Question: What do you think is the biggest burden for students when taking online classes?

Answer 1: Yes, I think so.

Answer 2: Yes, it is a burden because it is hard.

Answer 3: The biggest burden is making sure the internet works, because my connection is poor.

Answer 4: It seems that the biggest burden for many students is making sure the internet works. Specifically, though students may have internet at home, those who live in the countryside often don't have fast connections, and those with large families have to share the connection with many others, which slows down their connection. For example, in my house, we have Wi-Fi, but my father and my brother both use it for work, so my connection is often slow when watching videos such as class lectures.

The question is not a closed question, but Answer 1 gives a yes or no answer, making it completely inappropriate. Although Answer 2 seems to give an idea about what is a burden for students, it starts by answering "yes," which is inappropriate in response to an open question. Furthermore, the answer then only says that it is "hard," which means the same as "burden" and therefore does not provide much information. Answer 3 is an appropriate response to the question, but it gives little supporting information. In addition, the example is connected with the word "because" rather than vocabulary that marks examples, and there is an unclear connection between the personal example and why "making sure the internet works" is the biggest burden for students in general and not just the speaker. Answer 4 gives a very appropriate answer. It provides two points of evidence and connects the personal example to an explanation of why internet access might be a problem for other students as well. It also makes good use of the implicit phrase "it seems that" to avoid making the response seem overly opinionated.

B1.4 Phrasal Verbs and Idiomatic Expressions

Words and phrases that that are not interpreted according to their literal or dictionary meaning is referred to as "idiomatic." Though there are many types of idiomatic language, this chapter will introduce four: metaphors, phrasal verbs, idiomatic phrases, and idioms. Even though idiomatic language is not used extensively in written English, it is important to understand it because it is extremely common in spoken English – in everyday conversation and in academic presentations, lectures and classroom discussions. Becoming more familiar with how idiomatic language is used, in what situations it is used, and how to interpret it will greatly improve students' listening and speaking skills.

What to Know about Idiomatic Phrasal Verbs and Idiomatic Expressions

Students can approach learning English idiomatic language in several ways. The first way is to become familiar with, or develop some awareness of, some of the general cultural aspects and thinking of the native English-speaking world. This will help students recognize the situations and contexts in which idiomatic language is used. Another effective approach is to study the patterns and concepts by which idiomatic language is constructed. Doing so can improve students' ability to guess the actual meaning of idiomatic language when it is heard in context, even if the student has never heard the exact expression before. Finally, students can memorize some of the common idiomatic language charts below. This material, however, should be memorized using the knowledge of the patterns and concepts explained in this chapter.

Metaphors

Metaphors are expressions that are used to make a comparison between two things that are not completely alike but do have something in common. For example, the phrases "Life is a rollercoaster" and "She cried a river of tears" are metaphors. Of course, life is not actually a rollercoaster, but both have ups and downs. Likewise, tears are not rivers, but both tears and rivers consist of flowing water. Closely related to metaphors are similes. Similes are also idiomatic figures of speech that compare two things, but they use the words "like" or "as" to make it clear that the comparison is not literal. For example, "Life is a rollercoaster" is a metaphor, but "Life is **like** a rollercoaster" is a simile. Metaphors and similes are usually constructed based upon shared concepts that are often cultural. People who share these cultural concepts can make metaphorical comparisons easily and naturally, so understanding them (even if you don't agree with the concept) will help students to guess the meanings of English metaphors. The chart below contains English language cultural concepts and corresponding metaphor examples, as well as their meanings.

Cultural Concept	Metaphor Example	Meaning of Example
upward as positive	She's flying high in her new job.	She is doing very well in her new job.
downward as negative	He's been down in the dumps all day.	He's been depressed all day.
time as money	His mistake cost us 10 hours.	His mistake wasted 10 hours.
hardness as strength	She is my rock.	I rely on her for her strength.
argument as war	He shot my thesis full of holes.	He said my thesis was not valid.
sports as war	Our team was killed yesterday!	Our team lost yesterday.
life as a journey	Our relationship is at a crossroads.	We must decide how our relationship will continue.
ideas as items for sale	I'm not buying your story.	I don't believe your story.
effort as plants	All of our hard work has finally borne fruit.	Our hard work has finally led to good results.
things as people (personification)	Opportunity was knocking at my door.	I received an opportunity.
overstated descriptions (exaggeration)	A million people came to my house last night.	Many people came to my house last night.

Phrasal Verbs

Phrasal verbs consist of a verb and a preposition (such as "in," "on," "off") that together create a meaning different from that of the original verb. For example, the verb "catch" can mean "to grasp something with one's hands," and the preposition "on" means "physically in contact with something." However, when the two words are combined to make the phrasal verb "catch on," it can have the meaning "to come into contact with something and grasp it," but it can also have the meanings "to become popular" and "to become aware of something."

Phrasal verbs like this can have more than one meaning because prepositions themselves can have up to four different kinds of meanings: a location meaning, a motion meaning, a change meaning, or some other meaning. Most English learners are familiar with the location meaning of prepositions, because this is the most common. However, many learners may not be as familiar with the other three types of meanings, which are more idiomatic. By memorizing the common preposition meanings and understanding the relationship between the verb and preposition in most phrasal verbs, students can learn to guess the meanings of many phrasal verbs, even if they have never seen or heard them before. Look at the chart of common preposition meanings below and then read the explanation of how to guess the meanings of phrasal verbs based on these meanings.

Preposition	Motion Meaning	Change Meaning	Other Meaning
up	to move from a lower position to a higher one	to become more, better, higher, improved	to do completely, properly, or well
down	to move from a higher position to a lower one	to become less, worse, lower, degraded	to finish, realize, achieve or attain
in, into	to enter		
out (of)	to exit	to disappear, to appear	to do completely (causing something to be eliminated)
on, onto	to move to a position of touching	to become attached	to continue
off (of)	to move to a position of not touching	to become unattached	
back	to move to the original position or backwards	to return to original state	
away (from)	to move to a more distant position	to disappear	
after	to follow or chase		
under, below	to move to a lower position than something else		
over	to move to a higher position than something else or traverse it	to reverse, to become not standing	
across	to move from one side of something to the other		
along	to move on a set path or the same path as something else		to do something at the same time or together
around, about	to move in a circle, to move in various places near something		
through	to move in one side and then out of the other		
apart		to change from being whole to being in pieces	
together		to change from being in pieces to being whole	

In order to guess which meaning a preposition is taking in a phrasal verb, consider the type of verb. First, when the verb "be" is used, the preposition will usually take on the location meaning. "Be in," for instance, means "to be inside of something," such as in "The book is in the bag." However, if a verb of movement is used, for example "to run," "to fly," "to walk," the preposition will commonly take on a motion meaning. For instance, according to the chart above, the motion meaning of "in" is "to enter." Therefore, "run in" means "to enter by running," "jump in" means "to enter by jumping," and "fly in" means "to enter by flying." Similarly, when a verb that describes some kind of action or change is used in a phrasal verb, such as "to fade," or "to cut," the preposition will take on its change meaning, and the verb will describe how or why the change occurred. For example, according to the chart above, the change meaning of the preposition "away" is "to disappear." Therefore, when "away" is combined with the verb "fade," the meaning of the phrasal verb will then be "to disappear by fading." Likewise, "burn away" means "to make something disappear by the action of burning," and "wash away" means "to make something disappear by the action of washing." The chart below contains some of the common types of verbs that indicate location, motion, and change meanings.

common location meaning verbs	verbs of existing in a place: be, exist, sit, lay
common motion meaning verbs	1. simple verbs: go, come, get 2. verbs of self-motion: run, walk, roll, fly, jump 3. verbs of transportation: drive, fly, ride
common change meaning verbs	1. simple verbs: get, take, pick, turn, go, come*, fall* 2. action verbs: push, pull, put, set, kick, cut, flip, work 3. tools or instruments as verbs: glue, staple, tape, saw 4. onomatopoeia: click, knock, bump, smash, crack
common other meaning verbs	up = most verbs, but often those that take a positive meaning (e.g. clean, cheer, dress) down = verbs with negative connotations (e.g. close, break), verbs with clear goals (e.g. chase, hunt) out = verbs indicating a problem or mystery is being eliminated (e.g. figure out, find out, work out), verbs indicating a chance is being eliminated (e.g. miss out, strike out), verbs indicating stock is being eliminated (e.g. run out, sell out)

when "come" and "fall" are used as change verbs, they usually indicate that the change happened on its own, with no outside force or action

Though understanding the charts above and how prepositions and verbs can combine to create new meanings can help learners guess the meanings of many phrasal verbs, it is important to also be very familiar with some of the most common phrasal verbs. Below is a chart of the 32 most common phrasal verbs used in academic English. Students should learn the various meanings of these verbs. Many of the meanings can be explained through the charts above. For example, one of the meanings of "go out" is "to exit," because "go" is a simple verb that can indicate motion and the motion meaning of "out" is "exit." Furthermore, "go out" can also have the meaning "to disappear" because "go" can also be a simple verb indicating change and the change meaning of "out" is "disappear." However, students should be aware that some of the very common phrasal verbs in the chart below also have meanings that cannot be guessed based on the information above, and those meanings must simply be memorized. For example, "go out" can also have the meaning of "to have a romantic relationship with someone," which cannot be guessed simply based on the above charts.

work on	come out	carry out	get up
take on	go out	set out	pick up
get on/off	get out	get in[to]	take up
go on	turn out	go in	set up
carry on	point out	come back	end up
come on	find out	go back	follow up
go off	work out	get back	take over
go through	sort out	look after	go away

Idiomatic Phrases

The meanings of idiomatic phrases cannot be easily guessed using the aforementioned techniques. The chart below contains the 37 most common idiomatic phrases used in academic English. Please notice that some phrases contain the gender-neutral indefinite pronoun "one," meaning "a person." When using these idiomatic phrases, be sure to replace "one" with the appropriate specific definite pronoun. For instance, when using the idiomatic phrase "slip one's mind," "one's" must be changed to refer to the person being spoken about, as in "slip my mind," "slip your mind," "slip his mind," slip her mind," "slip Naoki's mind," and so forth.

Phrase	Meaning	Example Sentence
Time Related		
at some point	occurring at some time that is not exactly known or decided	I want you to check my paper at some point. When are you free?
at the time	occurring at the time being discussed	I didn't know you were a student at the time. I thought you had graduated by then.

so far	up to the current point in time, to a limited amount	So far, this is his best novel. Studying English will only take you so far. You'll have to actually use it to get better.
at the moment	right now	I'm busy at the moment, please come back later.
put time into	make effort, spend time doing	I put a lot of time into my project, so I got a good grade.

Opinions		
slip one's mind	to forget	I didn't go to the meeting because it slipped my mind.
point of view	one's opinion or feelings	His point of view is different from the rest of the team.
benefit of the doubt	to use a judgement despite uncertainty	I don't know if he was really sick or not, but I will give him the benefit of the doubt.
see what one is saying	to understand someone's opinion or idea	I see what you are saying, but I disagree.
shake one's head	to disagree or refuse	I asked if she would help, but she just shook her head.
beats me	to not know	A: What time does the meeting start? B: Beats me.
no doubt	it is certain	There is no doubt that the earth is round.
go for	to want	I could go for a break. I've been studying for 4 hours straight!

Cause and Effect		
lead to	to cause	Eating less and exercising more leads to weight loss.
bound to	will probably happen	With all the studying you have been doing, you are bound to pass the test.
in the event (of/that)	if something happens	In the event of rain, the game will be cancelled.

Work and Effort		
deal with	to take action, manage, handle, or treat	Only team leaders should deal with the administration office.
take advantage of	to make good use of an opportunity, to exploit	We should take advantage of the library while it is still open. He took advantage of my weakness.

take for granted	to fail to properly appreciate, to assume that something is true	I took my parent's generosity for granted. I took it for granted that I would be paid for my work.
for the sake of	the purpose or reason, in consideration of	My essay was not easy to understand, so I rewrote it for the sake of clarity. For the sake of other people's health, we should wear face masks when sick.
cut someone some slack	to allow more freedom or forgiveness than usual	Because he was sick, his teacher cut him some slack with the assignment deadline.
find oneself doing something	to do something naturally, without conscious intention	At her new job, she found herself applying the skills she had learned in university.
no matter what it takes	doing anything necessary to achieve something	He'll do whatever it takes to win, even cheat!
Interpersonal Feelings		
read between the lines	to find meaning that is not clearly stated, only implied	He said we had done enough, but reading between the lines, I knew that he thought we should have done more.
add insult to injury	to make a bad situation even worse	My boss not only said I could not get a pay increase in future, but to add insult to injury, he reduced my current pay.
hit it off	to form a good relationship with someone quickly	Luckily, I really hit it off with my new lab mate.
be in someone's shoes	to be in the same situation as someone	If I were in your shoes, I wouldn't drive in the heavy rain at night.
pull oneself together	to recover self-control and be calm	Bob was shocked after the car accident, but after he pulled himself together, he called the police.
on one's own	to receive no help	He asked for help with his paper, but I am busy, so he's on his own.
in touch with	to contact	Please keep in touch with your parents or else they will worry.
take it easy	to relax, to work at a comfortable pace	Hana took it easy after school today. A: I have so much to do today! B: Well, take it easy!
hang in there	to never give up	Maya didn't want to keep studying, but she hung in there and finally finished.

Amounts or Comparisons		
a good/great deal	many/much	Students at Tohoku University spend a good deal of their time in the library.
something like	approximately	Something like 500 people showed up to the festival.
by no means	absolutely not	Even though some people are late for class, it is by no means acceptable.
by all means	absolutely	A: May I have a look at your lab report? B: By all means.
as opposed to	in contrast to	Students here learn two foreign languages as opposed to other universities where they only learn English.

Idioms

The final type of idiomatic language discussed in this chapter is idioms. Idioms are similar to the idiomatic phrases above, but tend to have historical, cultural, literary, or proverbial origins. Below is a list of 20 common English idioms that often appear in everyday speech. As with idiomatic phrases, the gender-neutral indefinite pronoun "one" must be replaced with the proper specific definite pronoun when using these expressions.

Idiom	Meaning	Example Sentence
under the weather	feeling ill	I'm under the weather, so I won't be coming in to work today.
fall into one's lap	to get something luckily or coincidentally without effort	Good grades seem to fall into her lap for every class.
like the back of one's hand	to know something very well	I know Shinjuku like the back of my hand.
take the bull by the horns	to deal with a difficult situation in a very direct way	In this job, you'll have to take the bull by the horns.
take with a grain of salt	to not take something you are told seriously, because it may be untrue	I usually take the news that I read on Facebook with a grain of salt.
once in a blue moon	very rarely	I swim in the ocean once in a blue moon.
over one's head	too difficult to do	Those mathematical equations are easy for us but they are over the heads of our students.
call it a day	to stop working on something	We have completed enough work. Let's call it a day.

piece of cake	very easy	That test was a piece of cake.
let the cat out of the bag	to tell or reveal a secret	Please don't let the cat out of the bag about me moving to Tokyo.
get cold feet	to suddenly have the feeling of not wanting to do something that was planned	She's getting cold feet about her wedding tomorrow.
play by ear	to do something without a plan	I'm going to play this weekend by ear.
an arm and a leg	very expensive	The airfare to Europe costs an arm and a leg these days.
a far cry from	very different	The weather in Hawaii is a far cry from the weather in Hokkaido.
on the ball	to be attentive, and quick to act	Our new employee is really on the ball.
the straw that broke the camel's back	the last in a series of small bad things to happen that finally causes one big bad thing to happen	He was late again today – that was the straw that broke the camel's back. I'm going to have to fire him.
head over heels	to be in love, especially in the beginning of a relationship	He has been head over heels for her ever since they met.
on the fence	to be indecisive	He's sitting on the fence about attending a public or private university.
hit the sack hit the hay	go to sleep	I'm going to hit the sack around midnight.
hit the nail on the head	to do or say something perfectly	You really hit the nail on the head with your answer today.

Example of Phrasal Verbs and Idiomatic Expressions in Use

Look at the example conversations that contain the various types of idiomatic language (in **bold**) discussed above and answer the comprehension questions. A QR code is also provided at the end of the chapter that links to a recording of these examples.

MAN: Oh no! I spilled coffee on my white shirt! Is there any way I can get this stain to **come out**?

WOMAN: I'm not sure, but I don't think just putting it into the washing machine will clean it. You'll probably have to **steam it out.**

MAN: Steam it out? That's **over my head**.

WOMAN: Mine too. You'd better leave it to professionals. Do you want me to **drop it off** at the dry-cleaning shop for you?

1) What does the phrasal verb "come out" mean in this situation?

    (A) go back as before

    (B) come to the dry-cleaning shop

    (C) be removed

    (D) have coffee

2) How does the woman suggest the man clean the shirt?

    (A) by steaming it

    (B) by all means

    (C) with coffee

    (D) by washing it

3) What does the woman offer to do?

    (A) have coffee with the man

    (B) clean the man's shirt

    (C) drop the shirt

    (D) take the shirt to the dry-cleaning shop

In this context, "out" does not refer to the motion meaning "to exit." Instead, it takes on the change meaning "to disappear" or "to remove." Therefore, the answer to the first question is "C." The woman tells the man that the stain must be "steamed out" (made to disappear by steam). Therefore, the answer to the second question is "A." Finally, the woman offers to "drop it off." In this case, "off" takes on the change meaning of "become unattached." She will take the shirt and "drop" (leave) it at the dry-cleaning shop. Therefore, the answer to number 3 is "D."

> MAN: What do you think about this advertisement for a part-time job selling insurance policies? I could **go for** some extra money.
>
> WOMAN: I think applying would be a **waste of time.** You're always **searching for easy ways to make money,** but you should focus on something more stable. This job doesn't pay an hourly wage. It's all commission – you'll only get paid if you sell a lot of policies.
>
> MAN: I know, but it says there will opportunities for the position to **branch out** in the future.
>
> WOMAN: Perhaps. But I think this company will **take advantage of you** at the beginning. You may **find yourself working** hard for no pay.
>
> MAN: Well, I think that I'll **give** them **the benefit of the doubt.**
>
> WOMAN: OK. Why don't you try it out for a month or so? If you don't see **the fruits of your labor** by then you should quit.

1) What does the woman think will happen if the man applies for the job?
   (A) He will get the benefit of the doubt
   (B) He will search for an easier job
   (C) He won't make any money
   (D) He will work at a fruit farm

2) What is the man likely to do?
   (A) Take the advantages and disadvantages of the job
   (B) Quit the job after a month
   (C) Branch out in the future
   (D) Apply for the job

The man mentions that he wants extra money, but the woman does not think it is a good job and says that the employer will "take advantage" of him and that he may find himself "working hard for no pay." Therefore, the answer to number 1 is "C." The man says that he will "give them the benefit of the doubt," which means he will trust them, despite the woman's doubts. Therefore, the answer to the second question is "D."

English A2

Integrated Academic Reading and Writing

Objective 1: Attain the ability to identify the text's organization and logic

A2.1 Connotative and Denotative Meanings

A2.2 Suggestions, Inferences, and Implications

Objective 2: Acquire the ability to construct an academic paragraph

A2.3 Paragraph Writing

A2.4 Collocations

A2.1 Connotative and Denotative Meaning

Words have two types of meaning: denotative and connotative. The denotative meaning is the explicit or direct meaning of a word, sometimes referred to as the "dictionary meaning." On the other hand, the connotative meaning of a word is the feeling, implication or emotion that individuals, cultures and societies associate with a word. For example, the words "house" and "home" can both have the denotative meaning of "a place where people live." "House," however, only has the meaning of "a place where people live," whereas "home" can have the connotative meanings of "family," "belonging," "comfort," and "safety." Understanding both the denotation and connotation of words is important, as it will help students recognize an author's opinion and meaning to properly identify the argument. It is also important for understanding suggestions, inferences and implications (see Chapter A2.2). When reading academic articles, textbooks, and research papers for classes at Tohoku University, correctly noticing the differences between denotative and connotative meanings will improve students' reading comprehension, enabling them to understand the author's point of view and other biases the work may have.

What to Know about Connotative and Denotative Meaning

Dictionaries are the obvious resource to find the denotative meaning of a word. However, because connotations are cultural and changeable, and because there are only a few resource materials that readily list this type of information, determining a word's precise connotative meanings is slightly more difficult. There are three important aspects when identifying the connotation of a word: the degree of meaning, the positive or negative association and the context.

Degree of Meaning

Often, the connotation of a word has to do with the degree of meaning. For example, the following words all have a denotative meaning of "bad": "poor," "horrible," "awful," "terrible," "lousy," "unacceptable," and "atrocious." If, for example, a teacher used one of these words to describe a student's test results, how bad should the student understand the test results to have been? The words "unacceptable" and "poor" would probably indicate that the teacher recognizes the student's effort, but that it was simply not good enough compared to the rest of the class. In contrast, "lousy" or "awful" would indicate that the test was done without much effort. Words such as "terrible" and "horrible" would be even stronger, and, finally, "atrocious" indicates that the test results could not have been any worse. While all of these adjectives denotatively mean "bad," each has a particular degree of "bad" attached to it. In fact, most adjectives, adverbs and verbs have degrees of meaning attached to them. In order to find or guess the connotation of a word, find multiple examples of words with similar denotative meanings and compare the situations in which they are used.

Positive or Negative Association

Another aspect of connotative meaning is the positive or negative association that accompanies a word. For example, both the words "childlike" and "childish" have a denotative meaning of "young" or "immature." However, "childlike" can have a positive connotation, indicating innocence and sweetness. "Childish," on the other hand, usually means "foolish" and "badly behaved," and therefore has a more negative connotation.

In terms of culture, with respect to translating English and Japanese, it is important to remember that while words in each language may be easily translated denotatively, the connotative translations may be quite different. For example, it is possible to translate the word "jealousy" as the Japanese word "urayamashii," which can sometimes have a rather positive connotation. "Jealousy" in English, however, has a very negative connotation. This aspect is also true for some English loan words that are commonly used in Japanese. For example, the verb "to challenge," as used in Japanese, sometimes has the positive connotation of overcoming a problem and having a fighting spirit. In English, though it can also be understood in this way, it can also have the negative connotation of disagreeing with or fighting against someone.

In order to determine whether a word has a negative or positive connotation, find several examples of it used in context and make note of how often it is used in negative or positive situations. If it is used in both, then the connotation is likely neutral. However, if it primarily used in negative situations, it likely has a negative connotation and vice versa.

Context

The third aspect to consider when identifying the connotative meaning of a word is the context of the surrounding vocabulary. For example, the word "white," aside from describing the color of something, can also have several different connotative meanings. Depending on the surrounding context, "white" can refer to fear, sickness, innocence, boredom, weakness or cleanliness. Consider the following examples:

He suddenly went *white* with terror while climbing the high rocks. (fear)

After he ate the spoiled food, his face turned *white*. (sickness)

Looking at the four *white* walls everyday makes us all a little bit crazy. (boredom)

The losing army decided to surrender, so they raised a *white* flag. (weakness)

Those towels are as *white* as can be. (cleanliness)

Example of Connotative and Denotative Meaning in Use

In order to truly understand an author or speaker's opinion, main point or reason for writing or saying something, students need to be able to understand and identify the connotation of the words they use. For example, consider the following short passage and the questions that follow it. Notice how knowing the connotative meanings helps in comprehending the passage more accurately.

The story of the lost city of Atlantis is a famous one. However, it is just that – a story. Recently, I have been shocked at the number of scholars who have begun a naïve quest to prove that Atlantis was once a real place. Some of these researchers even provide flashy historical evidence, such as the fact that the famous Greek philosopher Plato often wrote about Atlantis. While I sympathize with the desire to discover that a land now considered mythical was once real, it is an absolute travesty that so many otherwise shrewd scholars would take this ridiculous Atlantis notion seriously.

1) What does the author think about Atlantis?
    (A) It is a shocking discovery.
    (B) There is plenty of evidence both for and against the idea that it was real.
    (C) The notion that Atlantis was a real place must be taken seriously.
    (D) It was not a real place.

2) What is the author's opinion of scholars who study Atlantis?
    (A) They are shrewd scholars.
    (B) She thinks they are foolish.
    (C) They are youthful and full of hope.
    (D) She is sympathetic that the researchers cannot convince others.

The answers are "D" and "B," respectively, for the following reasons: The author uses several words with negative connotations in this context to express the idea that some people still believe that Atlantis was once a real place. For example, she uses the words "naïve," "quest," "flashy," "travesty," and "ridiculous" to convey her strong feelings about the believability of this notion. She states that she thinks it is "just a story" and that she is critical of the idea. Therefore, she does not think Atlantis is a shocking discovery or that there is plenty of evidence on both sides (she describes the evidence as "flashy," which connotes that although it may look good, it does not have substance). Based on the connotations of the language used, we should know that she thinks that Atlantis was not a real place. Furthermore, though she sympathizes (i.e. she understands, but she does not agree) with researchers wanting to make important discoveries, she is clearly not trying to convince others that Atlantis was real. Further, she calls these scholars' goal "naïve," a word – in this context – with the negative connotative meaning of "inexperienced" and "easily fooled" and not the positive connotative meanings of "youthful "or "hopeful" that the word "naïve" may have in different contexts. She does mention that many (not all) of the scholars are "otherwise shrewd." This means that she thinks they are shrewd about other topics but not about Atlantis. Finally, her use of words like "travesty" and "ridiculous," which have negative connotations, further reinforces the notion that she thinks that the study of Atlantis has no merit.

A2.2 Suggestions, Inferences, and Implications

An implication is something an author or speaker communicates indirectly through hints, clues or hedged wording (see Chapter B2.2). A suggestion is usually some type of advice or expression of opinion, but one that is given by means of an implication. An inference is a logical conclusion that we can draw about an assumption or suggestion based on the available information, even though it is not explicitly stated. For example, if you make dinner for your friends and one says, "you could be a gourmet cook," they are implying that the food is delicious because they are comparing you to a gourmet cook, thus indicating that the food is good without ever saying so directly. Similarly, if your friends all ask for seconds, you can infer that the meal was delicious, because they probably would not ask for more if it was bad. Recognizing suggestions and implications and making inferences is important for understanding the logic of a text because it will help you to understand the author's true message and what information you should get from the text. Making inferences will be important for you when reading academic texts at Tohoku University for your classes, having discussions, or when figuring out which answer is correct on a standardized test.

What to Know about Suggestions, Inferences, and Implications

There are three main skills that will help you to make inferences: understanding the author's certainty about a statement, comprehending the logical connection between pieces of information, and figuring out why the author included certain information.

Degree of Certainty

As discussed in Chapter A2.1, words can have both denotations and connotations, which can change the feeling of a text. Recognizing how strong a word is and whether it has a positive or negative connotation is one important way to catch an author's implications and suggestions about a certain topic. However, the author can also use words to show how sure they are about a statement or how likely they think it is to be true. One way to do this is with adverbs such as "probably," "unlikely," or "possibly," and another way is the use of modal verbs. Though modal verbs often take one of their primary meanings, they also often help to imply how sure the author is about something or how likely they think it is to be true. Learn the meanings in the following chart and how they can affect the meanings of sentences.

Modal Verb	Standard Meaning	Implication
Will	Future tense	100% sure
Would	Imaginary situation / past future tense	About 90% sure
Must	Need	80% and there is evidence
Shall	Suggestion / decision	X
Should	Better to do	About 70% sure
May	Permission	About 50% sure
Might	X	A little less than 50% sure
Can	Ability	(rarely used here)
Could	Past ability / imaginary situation	Low possibility

MAN: Will your brother come to the party tonight?

WOMAN: -He will come (100% planning on coming)

-He should be coming (he probably will come, but it is not certain)

-He may come (there is about a 50% chance of him coming)

-He might come (the chances that he will not come are slightly higher)

-He could come (there is a very low chance that he will come)

Logical Connection

Understanding the connection between sentences, details, or pieces of information is also important for making correct inferences or catching an author's implication. The major types of logical connections are chronological (one action happened before/after another), conjunction (both actions happened), disjunction (only one action happened), implication (an action will happen conditionally), and cause/effect (one action happens because of another). Students must know the following common ways to mark these logical connections.

Connection	Words	Meaning / Inference
chronological	next, after, later, and then, subsequently, followed by	One thing happened after another (not caused)
	before, preceded by	One thing happened before another (not caused)
conjunction	and, and then, moreover, furthermore	Both are happening
	but, however, although, even though, in spite of, nevertheless, yet	Both are happening (one is not expected in the circumstances)
disjunction	either, or, either but not both, instead, rather	Only one is happening (but not both, and not none)

— 63 —

implication	if, then	One thing can only happen if some condition is fulfilled
	no…without	One thing cannot happen if some condition is not fulfilled
	implies, suggests, points to	One thing MIGHT mean another (but we cannot be 100% sure)
cause/effect	because, since, therefore, so, due to, on account of, seeing that, causes, leads to, brings about, yields	One thing happened as a result of the other (the second thing cannot happen without the first thing)
	in order to, so as to, so that, to, for the purpose of	One thing happened for the purpose of causing the second

Understanding Why Information is Included

Finally, understanding why the author has included certain information will help you to make inferences about what the main points and supporting details are. As pointed out in Chapters B2.1 and A1.4, texts and speeches generally have main ideas. These main ideas are usually found in the first sentences of written paragraphs and are supported by many kinds of details. These details may also be supported by even smaller details. Some of the common ways to provide these details are (1) illustrating with examples, (2) explaining or describing, (3) supporting with evidence or giving reasons, and (4) contrasting or refuting opposing ideas. If you can identify the main idea in a paragraph or speech, you can then try to figure out how it connects to the other sentences. This will help you to determine the author's viewpoint and what they are arguing for or against. Study the chart of words and phrases that are often used for each of these purposes so that you can recognize them if you see them in a text. However, please be careful: sentences are not always clearly marked with these types of words, so you might have to use your other skills and knowledge of writing organization to determine the relationship between two sentences.

Examples	Explaining/describing	Evidence	Contrasting/refuting
illustrates/depicts/ exemplifies…	This means that…	For one…	…misses/ takes for granted/ misinterprets…
For example, … / such as…	In other words…	…provides/gives support for…	…doesn't take <something> into account
…including X, Y, Z.	because/so/therefore/…	…shows that…	However/but/though/while/contrary to
…from X to Z	specifically/i.e.	…is clear from the fact that…	

Example of Suggestions, Implications, and Inferences in Use

In order to fully understand a passage, you will need to make assumptions based on the information given. For example, consider the following short passage and the questions that follow it. The answers are not given directly, but we can infer them.

Compounds, substances that are made when two or more elements are chemically bonded together, are important for both our bodies and the devices that we use to make life easier. However, different compounds are important for different reasons. While there are many different categories of compounds, one of the most important distinctions is based on whether or not a compound is organic.

The first and most important difference between organic and inorganic compounds has to do with the presence or absence of a carbon atom. In general, if a compound contains a carbon atom, it is organic. If it does not contain a carbon atom, it is instead classified as an inorganic compound. For example, sucrose, better known as sugar, contains carbon, which causes it to be classified as an organic compound. However, there are some exceptions, such as carbon dioxide. Carbon dioxide could be classified as organic, because it contains a carbon atom, but this does not take into account the fact that the amount of carbon in this compound is not large enough to form strong bonds with the oxygen in the molecule.

Another important distinction is that organic compounds are associated with living things, while inorganic compounds are not. This means that organic compounds will usually be found in plants, animals, and even bacteria. In contrast, although some living things might contain inorganic compounds, they are usually present in only very small amounts.

1) What does the author think about carbon dioxide?
    (A) It is a better example of an organic compound than sucrose.
    (B) It is a clear guideline for differentiating inorganic and organic compounds.
    (C) It should not be considered an organic compound.
    (D) It does not take into account the weak bonds with oxygen in the molecule.

2) Why did the author include the last sentence?
    (A) To describe the association between living things and organic compounds
    (B) To refute the idea that inorganic compounds are found in living things
    (C) To explain why carbon is necessary in living things
    (D) To give an example of living things

In the example above, the author says that carbon dioxide could be classified as organic, indicating that he is not very sure of this claim. Then, he gives reasons why it should not be considered organic, which allows us to understand that he does not think it should be considered an organic compound ("C"). He is also clearly showing that carbon dioxide is an exception to the carbon-atom rule, so carbon dioxide is not associated with being a clear guideline for differentiating between organic and inorganic compounds, nor is it a better example of an organic compound. Furthermore, "D" repeats words from the passage, but the subject "it" (= carbon dioxide) does not match the verb "take into account." People, ideas, or theories do or do not take things into account, but not inanimate (non-living) objects. A correct expression would be "the idea that carbon dioxide is organic does not take into account the weak bonds with oxygen in the molecule."

The reason the speaker gives the last sentence is ("A") to describe the association between living things and organic compounds. If we follow the logical order of ideas presented, we can see that this information is no longer related to "carbon" ("C") and is instead talking about whether or not these compounds are found in living things "A." The speaker's words do not refute the idea that inorganic compounds are found in living things ("B") and in fact show that it is sometimes possible. Furthermore, the words "this means that" are often associated with explaining, describing, or possibly providing evidence, but are not for giving examples ("D") or contrasting ("B").

A2.3 Paragraph Writing

A paragraph contains a series of related sentences that describe a single topic. Longer pieces of writing such as research reports, essays, and theses, contain a series of related paragraphs that develop the various single topics into one coherent theme. The ability to write a good paragraph must be mastered in order to write longer papers effectively (see Chapter C1.1), so this is an essential skill that students will need in their academic careers at Tohoku University, because students in all departments will at some point be expected to write English papers, essays, and research reports. Furthermore, because English paragraphs have a uniform structure, understanding their components can also improve reading comprehension. For example, recognizing a paragraph's structure gives clues about where keywords, topic sentences and supporting information is located, which helps with skimming and scanning (see Chapter A1.3). This is also important for Tohoku University students who must also take standardized English exams and read dense, technical English textbooks.

What to Know about Paragraph Writing

There are three main things to keep in mind when writing a paragraph: structure, transition vocabulary, and variation.

Paragraph Structure

Academic English paragraphs share a similar structure. Well-organized paragraphs start with an introductory sentence called a topic sentence, which describes the main idea of the paragraph. The topic sentence is followed by several supporting sentences, which further develop the idea, and the paragraph ends with either a concluding or a transition sentence. A paragraph should be unified, in that all the sentences should support the main idea as presented in the topic sentence. A coherent paragraph is one in which each sentence flows smoothly into the next sentence without shifting to irrelevant or unrelated information. A good paragraph also clearly connects previous information with new information. The basic structure of a paragraph is shown here:

1. Topic Sentence

2. Supporting Sentence 1
    Supporting Sentence 2
    …etc.

3. Concluding Sentence

The Topic Sentence

The topic sentence clearly states the topic, purpose, or main idea of the paragraph. When writing a topic sentence, it is important that the idea not be too general, otherwise, the topic may not be able to be discussed in a single paragraph. On the other hand, it is equally important that the idea not be too specific, otherwise, supporting information to further develop the topic may be unnecessary. Compare the following topic sentence examples:

(A) Fairness is one of the benefits associated with Japanese school uniforms.
(B) Japanese school uniforms reflect various aspects of Japanese culture.
(C) Japanese school uniforms, adopted in the Meiji era, violate the human right of self-expression.
(D) My Japanese school uniform is very stylish.

"A" is a good topic sentence because it is neither too general nor too specific. It clearly expresses the idea that fairness is a benefit of school uniforms. It invites supporting information by indicating that there are other benefits of school uniforms. "B" is too general to be a topic sentence because it does not mention any aspects of Japanese culture around which the paragraph can be built. This means that multiple paragraphs will be needed to develop the topic. "C" is a poor topic sentence because it includes two main ideas, which need to be separated into at least two paragraphs. "D" expresses a personal opinion rather than an idea that could be expanded upon, so it is not a very good topic sentence either.

Supporting Sentences

Supporting sentences further develop the idea captured in a topic sentence. Supporting sentences can provide *evidence* for the main idea or *clarification* of the main idea. Evidence includes reasons, examples, statistics, and other factual data that support the idea. Clarifications include explanations, definitions of important terms, and classifications. If a paragraph's supporting sentences are irrelevant or only weakly connected to the topic sentence, the paragraph will be unclear. When writing a paragraph, ensure that all sentences relate clearly to the topic sentence. If they do not, then a new paragraph will need to be written for those sentences.

Concluding and Transition Sentences

Concluding sentences and transition sentences do not present new information, but either summarize the important points of the paragraph with a concluding sentence or lead the reader to the next paragraph with a transition sentence. Transition sentences are necessary to connect the idea presented in one paragraph to a new idea presented in the next paragraph. In contrast, concluding sentences are required at the end of a section (see Chapter C1.1).

Transition Vocabulary

In academic writing, particular transitional vocabulary and phrases are used to show both the logical connections between ideas and to introduce supporting sentences that provide evidence for and clarification of ideas. Please refer to Chapter A2.2 for a complete list of the transition vocabulary used to make logical connections. The chart below, however, lists common words and phrases that are used in academic writing to introduce supporting sentences that provide evidence and clarification. Students who memorize the transition vocabulary listed in both Chapter A2.2 and in the chart below will be able to create longer, more descriptive sentences that more clearly demonstrate the relationship between ideas.

Introducing Reasons	it should be noted that; due to (the fact that); is based on; it follows that; factors; consequently; the reason for/why…; for one
Introducing Examples	for instance; for example; to illustrate; as can be seen by; including…; such as…; in the case that…; (e.g. <list>)
Introducing Numbers	a wide range of; there are a number of; as a matter of fact; the results/chart/ study show(s) that
Introducing Counter-arguments	while/though…; on the other hand; does not take into account; but at the same time
Providing Explanation	Specifically; in other words; with respect to; as explained by; (i.e.); this means that; (be) considered as
Providing Definitions	(be) regarded as; means, meaning; also known as; what is called…; refers to
Providing Classification	to distinguish between; the difference between; fall into; divide into; categorize

Variation

In English writing, it is important not to overuse the same words or phrases in a single paragraph or sentence. Good writers make use of a variety of words and phrases to better illustrate their ideas. Using synonyms (see Chapter A1.2) and paraphrases (see Chapter A1.4) instead of repeating words and phrases used earlier in the paragraph can help improve variation and increase clarity.

Example of Paragraph Writing in Use

Read the paragraph below. Notice how it follows the general paragraph structure outlined above, makes good use of transition vocabulary (in **bold**) and employs synonyms for variation.

Hydraulic fracturing, **also known as** fracking, can bring great economic benefit to local communities, but environmental drawbacks outweigh these potential benefits. Hydraulic fracturing **refers to** the process by which highly pressurized water, sand, ceramic beads, and a mixture of chemicals are injected deep into the ground, causing subterranean rock formations to crack and **subsequently** release the natural gas and oil deposits they contain. **It should be noted that** fracking is highly effective **with respect to** mining otherwise out-of-reach oil and gas and thereby does well to increase the supplies of much-needed fossil fuels. **In addition**, fracking is labor-intensive and therefore its mining operations provide hundreds of jobs to the local communities near fracking sites. **However,** these advantages **do not take into account** the environmental hazards posed by this mining method. **For one,** there is the highly publicized issue of earthquakes being caused by the reinsertion into the ground of wastewater from the fracking process. These man-made seismic events have been recorded in virtually every location where hydraulic fracturing has taken place. **Furthermore,** once a fracking well has run dry, the chemical-laden fluids remain behind, contaminating the surrounding soil and **bringing about** serious health risks. **Specifically,** more than two dozen chemicals, including toluene, ethylbenzene, and xylene, which are proven carcinogens, are used in this mining process. **Moreover,** fracking causes airborne pollutants to be released into the atmosphere, which compromises the air quality in the region. **For instance,** dangerous amounts of methane, sulfur oxide, and benzene have been recorded at fracking locations. **Therefore,** more rules, regulations, and safeguards need to be instituted before hydraulic fracturing can be considered as a viable option for unearthing petroleum products.

In this example, the topic sentence clearly outlines the idea that the disadvantages of fracking outweigh any advantages it may have. The supporting sentences plainly define the topic and give examples that support the idea. The paragraph uses transition vocabulary from both this chapter and the logical connections list in Chapter A2.2. In addition, there is variation in the paragraph's vocabulary and style. For example, though there are few synonyms for "fracking," the paragraph uses several variations to describe the water used in fracking, such as "fluid," "wastewater," and "hydraulic." The words "process," "method," and "unearth" are used to discuss the concept of mining. Further, the paragraph uses "fossil fuels" and "petroleum products" as synonyms for "oil and natural gas." Finally, the paragraph concludes with a transitional sentence that allows the next paragraph to introduce the new idea of specific rules and regulations related to fracking.

A2.4 Collocations

Collocations are particular words or phrases that are usually, if not always, paired together with other particular words or phrases. Native English speakers use and expect these pairings, and different pairings may sound unnatural or be grammatically incorrect. For example, the verb "commit," meaning "to do," usually goes with words that have negative connotations, such as "crime," "mistake," or other words that may describe a negative action. Therefore, one says, "commit a robbery" or "commit a terrible act," but cannot say, "commit tennis" or "commit shopping." Learning collocations is important because not using them correctly – in both speaking and writing – will cause communication problems. Also, it is important for Tohoku University students to recognize collocations when encountering them in academic lectures and textbooks because this will help them to process the English more quickly and easily. For example, the verb "pose," meaning "to cause" or "to present," will often go with nouns that have a negative or difficult connotation, such as "threat," "problem," or "question," so when reading something like "This situation poses a …," students can reasonably expect one of these types of words to follow.

What to Know about Collocations

The first step is to recall common collocations that use the four most basic English verbs, namely "do," "have," "make," and "take." Simple examples include "do homework," "have a party," "make a friend," and "take a test." Other collocations use less common verbs such as "break," "save," "tell," "catch," and "pay," as in "break a promise," "save space," "tell a joke," "catch a chill," and "pay attention," and must simply be memorized.

When memorizing collocations, it is important to determine whether the construction has a negative or positive connotation (see Chapter A2.1), as exemplified by the verbs "commit" and "pose" in the examples in the opening paragraph. For example, the noun "scheme," meaning "a plan," often has a negative connotation, and can thus be used in collocations with negative meanings. The verb "plot," meaning "to make a plan," is an example of a collocation that usually takes a negative word, and thus the collocation "plot a scheme" can be created, which suggests that the plan is likely illegal, wrong or badly intentioned. In contrast, the verb "formulate," also means "to make," but is usually not used with words that have negative connotation. Thus, the collocation "formulate a plan" can be created, which suggests that the plan that is positive, useful, or good. However, it would sound strange to say "formulate a scheme" or "plot a plan."

List of the Most Common Academic Collocations by Headword

The list below represents the most common in academic English. The words in (parentheses) are generally needed but not required in all circumstances.

Headword	Common Collocations
achieve	achieve a goal, achieve an objective, achieve an outcome
address	address an issue
adopt	adopt (an) approach, adopt (a) procedure, be widely adopted
arrangement	make arrangements
attempt	make an attempt
authority	exercise authority (over <someone>)
clue	give a clue, provide a clue (about <something>)
collect	collect data, collect information
comment	make a comment (about <something>)
commit	commit an offense, commit a crime, commit to memory, commit to <doing something>
conduct	conduct research, conduct an experiment, conduct a survey
conference	attend a conference, hold a conference
convey	convey a message, convey information, convey (a) meaning
correct	correct an error, correct a mistake
deal	deal with (an issue/problem/etc.)
deem	deem (in)appropriate, deem necessary
demonstrate	demonstrate competence, be (clearly) demonstrated
doubt	cast doubt on <something>
engage	engage in (an activity)
enhance	(greatly) enhance performance
face	face a challenge, face a dilemma, face a problem, face difficulty, face discrimination
fall into	fall into the category (of), fall into a number of categories
follow	follow instructions, follow the law, follow the rules
format	follow a format, use a format, standard format
gain	gain access (to), gain information, gain insight (into)
impression	create an impression, make an impression give <someone> an impression
initial	initial period, initial phase, initial stage
insight	gain insight, give insight, offer insight, provide insight (into)
interview	conduct an interview
judgment	make a judgment
message	convey a message, deliver a message

obligation	have an obligation, fulfill an obligation
observation	make a/an (direct) observation
obtain	obtain a result, obtain data, obtain information
opportunity	create an opportunity, offer an opportunity, provide an opportunity
overview	provide an overview, give an overview
parameter	set (the) parameters
perform	perform a function, perform an operation, perform a task
pose	pose a challenge, pose a problem, pose a question, pose a threat (to)
precede	take precedence (over), preceding chapter, preceding section
present	present an argument, present a challenge, present a summary, present data, present evidence
presentation	give a presentation
priority	give priority (to)
procedure	adopt a procedure, follow a procedure, use a procedure
raise	raise an issue, raise a question, raise awareness
range	cover a range (of), the entire range (of), the full range (of)
reach	reach an agreement, reach consensus, reach a peak
recommend	make a recommendation
refer	be (commonly) referred to (as)
regard	be (widely) regarded (as)
rely	rely on
require	meet a (minimum) requirement
research	conduct research (on), carry out research (on)
resemblance	bear a resemblance (to), bear no resemblance (to)
resolve	resolve (a) conflict, resolve a dispute
responsible	accept responsibility (for), assume responsibility (for), take responsibility (for), be (directly /partly/primarily) responsible (for)
result	obtain a result, result in
role	play a role, take on a role, assume the role (of), take the role (of)
seek	seek help, seek information
seem	seem (in)appropriate, seem obvious, seem plausible
sense	in a (literal/figurative) sense
serve	serve a function
set	set a goal, set an objective, set the agenda, set the parameters
strategy	develop a strategy, have a strategy
suit	be suited to, be suited for
support	support an argument
task	carry out a task, complete a task, perform a task

technique	develop a technique, employ a technique, use a technique
tendency	exhibit a tendency, have a tendency, show a (strong) tendency (to)
theory	develop a theory, test a theory
topic	cover a topic, discuss a topic, related topic, research topic
treatment	give <someone> (preferential/special) treatment, receive treatment
vested	(have a) vested interest in <something>

List of Commonly Misused Collocates

Below is a list of words that are often used together incorrectly by Japanese learners of English.

Headword	Incorrect Collocation and Explanation
by	cut ~~by~~ scissors ("With" should be used for tools or instruments.)
challenge	~~challenge~~ a solution to the problem ("Challenge" cannot be used for attempts. Instead, use the word "try.")
grow	grow vs. grow up ("Grow" is transitive and not used for humans; e.g. He grew his hair long. "Grow up" is intransitive and can be used for humans; e.g. He grew up in Germany)
how	~~How~~ do you think? (The correct question word here is "what")
meet	~~meet an accident~~ ("Get into an accident" or "have an accident" is most often used.)
narrow	His apartment is too ~~narrow~~. ("Narrow" is not generally used for rooms or buildings. The sentence above should use "small." However, "narrow" can be used for corridors, hallways and other paths.)
open	~~open a meeting~~ (meetings usually take "have," whereas "open" a meeting actually means "start" a meeting)
play	~~play running/skiing/etc.~~ ("Play" is usually only used for sports that use a ball, or that are games that have scored points. Most other sporting activities such as races, judged competitions, track and field, etc. use "do." For certain sports, the name of the sport itself becomes the verb, i.e. I ski, I figure skate, I surf. Some martial arts, however, may also use the verb; "practice," i.e. I practice karate.)

to	attend ~~to~~ class, turn ~~to~~ cold, go ~~to~~ back home, walk ~~to~~ up the stairs ("To" is unnecessary after these verbs)
wish	I ~~wish~~ he will win. (Use "hope" for desires that are possible or likely to happen, and "wish" for desires that are impossible or unlikely to happen.)
with	marry ~~with~~ \<someone\>, date ~~with~~ \<someone\> ("With" is not required in these phrases)

Examples of Collocations in Use

Please read the following passage and choose the correct words to fill in the blanks. Notice that the answers can only be found by reviewing the collocations listed above.

One of the greatest feats ever accomplished by humankind was successfully landing on the Moon and returning to Earth. Many people perhaps think of this achievement as the result of the natural advancement of knowledge, science and technology over time.

The underlying story, however, is not that simple. One rationale for both the United States and the Soviet Union ___ (1) ___ the **goal** of going to the Moon in the late 1950s came from the tensions of the Cold War. During this time, hostilities between the United States and the Soviet Union ran high, and the two rival nations constantly ___ (2) ___ **attempts** to ___ (3) ___ the **impression** that their respective nation was the most dominant military power in the world.

In order to do this, both countries ___ (4) ___ top **priority** to their weapons and rocket programs, which resulted in tremendous progress in the area of manned space flight. Today, the entire world enjoys the benefits of those initial efforts, but it is somewhat unfortunate that these technological advances came about, in part, as a result of the two nations attempting to extend their militaristic influence across the globe.

1) (A) looking   (B) setting   (C) aiming   (D) targeting
2) (A) had   (B) made   (C) tried   (D) aimed
3) (A) create   (B) have   (C) present   (D) show
4) (A) gave   (B) allowed   (C) did   (D) ordered

Answers: 1 = "B," 2 = "B," 3 = "A," 4 = "A"

Most of these can be found in the list of common academic collocations above. Number 2 can also be found on the list of commonly misused collocations.

English B2

Integrated Academic Speaking and Listening

Objective 1: Develop pragmatic competence

B2.1 Tone of Voice
B2.2 Speech Acts

Objective 2: Acquire the ability to discuss various topics

B2.3 Fluency and Pronunciation
B2.4 Discussion Strategies

B2.1 Tone of Voice

Tone of voice is how a speaker says their words. It is often used as a clue that they should be understood figuratively or indirectly, which makes understanding tone of voice important for understanding a speaker's intended meaning or purpose correctly. The ability to interpret a speaker's tone of voice and how it affects their meaning is necessary to understand spoken implications (see Chapter A2.2). Therefore, this skill is important for students at Tohoku University when discussing research, listening to lectures and presentations, and requesting information.

What to Know about Tone of Voice

In order to understand how a speaker's tone of voice affects their meaning, students must first become aware of the types of changes to tone of voice, how it can express attitude, that it often signals figurative language, and the types of implied meaning that are possible due to tone of voice being added to single words in a sentence.

Types of Changes to Tone of Voice

Tone of voice can be signaled in a number of ways. The first is word stress, which is when additional power or loudness is added to an entire word (as opposed to the natural stress that occurs on certain syllables in certain words). Stress is often coupled with a pause either before or after the stressed word. The next change in tone of voice is called stretching, which is when the vowel sound of a word is extended. The final type deals with changing the pitch of a word or phrase. Word stress and stretching are often used to signal figurative language or implied meaning (see the sections below), but changes in pitch can express a variety of meanings.

Pitch and Attitude

One of the purposes of rising or falling pitch is to mark important words. For example, increases and decreases in pitch are often used in the presentation of lists. Specifically, the items being listed generally have a rising pitch, and then falling pitch is used to signal the last item in the list. However, pitch can also be used to show a speaker's intent. For example, consider the simple sentence, "You went." If this were a statement, both words would usually be pronounced with a similar tone of voice, but if the pitch increases with the word "went," the sentence is understood to be a question: "You went?" Finally, pitch also gives clues about a speaker's attitude towards a statement, word, or the general situation. Falling or lower pitch will usually be used with words that speakers feel negatively towards or when they are generally unhappy. Conversely, rising or higher pitch is used with words that speakers feel positively towards or when they are excited or happy. Recognizing this allows listeners to interpret or guess what the speaker wants to say. For example, consider the sentence, "Oh, you got a blue one." If it is said with a flat pitch, we can suppose that the speaker is simply noticing that the object is blue and does not particularly care about the color. However, if it is said with a low pitch and a falling pitch on the word "blue," we would assume that they are unhappy about the object, particularly because of the color. The reverse would be true if the same sentence were spoken with a high pitch and a rising pitch on the word "blue:" we would think that the speaker was happy about the object because it is blue.

Figurative Language and Tone of Voice

If word stress or stretching is used, it often signals that the word or phrase is taking a figurative meaning (i.e. a secondary, less common, or indirect meaning). For example, as discussed in Chapter A2.2, the word "could" can take the meaning of "was able to" or "low possibility." If someone is invited to a party and they say "I could go," adding word stress or stretching to "could," they are probably indicating that the less common or metaphorical meaning (i.e. probably not) is being used and thus are probably trying to politely refuse. Similarly, "I don't know" can simply mean that the speaker does not have information. However, if stretching is applied to the word "know," this indicates that the speaker is politely saying "no," as illustrated by the two responses from the woman in the example conversation below:

> MAN: Will you help Professor Tanaka with his research project?
> WOMAN: I don't know. (she is not sure; perhaps she has not been asked or is considering whether or not she will)
> WOMAN: I don't **knooooow**. (she is trying to say she probably will not or does not want to)

Two common types of figurative language that are often marked by word stress and stretching are exaggeration, which means to describe something as bigger, better, worse or more important than it actually is (see Chapter B1.3); and sarcasm, which is when the speaker's words should be understood to have the opposite meaning. These techniques are generally not used in academic writing because without tone of voice to mark them, they can be unclear and cause confusion. However, they are an integral part of spoken English, and thus students should strive to recognize them. The following are examples:

> He drank **100 liters** of water after the race! (Exaggeration; he drank a lot of water)
> That's a **greeeaaaat** idea. (Sarcasm; the speaker thinks it is a bad idea)

Implied Meaning and Tone of Voice

Tone of voice can also be used to create implied meaning. In other words, it can be used to mark words or phrases that the listener should guess carry additional meaning, without being directly told what this meaning is. Though the additional meaning depends on the context and which word in the sentence is stressed, the stressed word is the key to understanding the implied meaning. In standard positive sentences, the implication is that the stressed word, and not some other one, is true, which often signals that the speaker previously misunderstood something about the word or is surprised by that particular piece of information. Therefore, in the example sentence below, "You walked to the store," the speaker may have misheard who had walked to the store or have been confused or surprised about who had done the action.

Positive Statements

Sentence	Implication
You walked to the store.	(none)
You walked to the store.	You walked to the store – not any other person.
You *walked* to the store.	You walked to the store – you did not go by any other means of transportation.
You walked to the *store*.	You walked to the store – not to any other location.

In negative sentences, the stressed word indicates what in the sentence makes it false, so we can probably assume the other parts of the sentence are true. Therefore, in the example sentence below, "*I* don't want a book," the speaker wants to indicate that everything about the statement (i.e. wanting a book) is true, except for the stressed information (i.e. the person who wants it). Therefore, we can assume that someone wants a book, but it is not the speaker (i.e. "I").

Negative Statements

Sentence	Implication
I don't want a book.	(none)
I don't want a book.	Someone else wants a book, not the speaker.
I don't want *a* book.	The speaker wants books, not just one book.
I don't want a *book*.	The speaker wants something, but not a book.

In questions, the stressed word indicates what the speaker is calling into question. Speakers often use stress to clarify their intention if they have asked a question and have not received the information they desire. Therefore, in the example sentence below, "*What* is in the blue bag?," the speaker probably received other information, such as where the blue bag is or whose bag it is, but did not understand or find out what object is inside of it.

Positive Questions

Sentence	Implication
What is in the blue bag?	(none)
What is in the blue bag?	Other information was received, but not exactly what the contents are.
What is **in** the blue bag?	Information was received about what is outside the bag, but not inside.
What is in the **blue** bag?	Information was received about what is inside another bag, but not the blue one.
What is in the blue **bag**?	Information was received about what is inside something blue, but not the blue bag.

In negative questions, the stressed word often indicates not only what is in question but also the thing that makes the premise false. Therefore, in the example sentence below, "Why don't *you* help me?," it is clear that the *reason* the speaker is asking the question is that the premise (the addressee helps the speaker) is not true, and the thing that makes it not true is the subject (i.e. the addressee – "you"). Thus, we can assume that the rest of the premise is true (i.e. that some people help the speaker – "me"), just not the subject ("you").

Negative Questions

Sentence	Implication
Why don't you help me?	(none)
Why don't **you** help me?	Others help me, but only you do not.
Why don't you help **me**?	You help others, but not me.
Why don't **you** help **me**?	I often help you, but you never help me.
Why don't you **help** me?	You do other things but never help.

Examples of Tone of Voice in Use

Look at the example conversation and then try to guess the answers to the questions. A QR Code linked to a recording of the conversation and the other examples is provided at the end. Notice how pragmatic competence and knowledge of tone of voice are necessary to understand the examples correctly.

> WOMAN: Do you want to work on the homework assignment together?
> MAN: *Again*?! You shouldn't ask me all the time. You will never pass the test if *you* don't do your homework sometimes.
> WOMAN: I don't ask *all of the time*.

1) Why does the man not want to help the woman?
   (A) He thinks she should study harder.
   (B) He thinks she should try doing the homework by herself.
   (C) He is tired of always being asked.
   (D) He does not have time.

2) What can be inferred about the woman?
   (A) She does not work very hard.
   (B) She never does her homework.
   (C) She often studies together with others.
   (D) She will never pass the test.

In the example above, the man changes his tone of voice at "again," implying that he is surprised by the woman's request, probably because she makes this request often. He then makes an implication with a positive statement by adding word stress to "you," implying that she should do the homework by herself (i.e. not with someone else). The woman changes her tone of voice in a negative statement, which means that she accepts the statement is true with the exception of the stressed words (i.e. "all of the time"). This means that the only thing that is untrue about the statement is that she does it "all of the time," so we know that she does do it sometimes. Therefore, we know that the man thinks that the woman should try doing the homework by herself ("B"), and that the woman often (but not always) studies together with others ("C"). However, we cannot know whether the man has time, nor whether the woman works hard, because these things are never mentioned. Furthermore, we do not know whether she will pass the test, because this is in the future, and we do not know what actions she will take.

B2.2 Speech Acts

Speech acts are utterances (spoken words) used to accomplish a specific goal (e.g. suggesting, requesting, refusing, apologizing, promising, ordering, asserting, etc.). To properly perform and understand a speech act, both speakers and listeners need to be aware of the situation, the speaker's intention, and the purpose of the speech act. Speech acts may be direct, in which case it is usually clear what the speaker is communicating. However, speech acts may also be indirect, which sometimes makes them seem unclear and forces the listener to think carefully about the speaker's true objective. The ability to recognize speech acts is an important language skill that Tohoku University students will need when writing research proposals and reporting research data with an appropriate level of uncertainty, and talking with teachers and students with an appropriate level of politeness.

What to Know about Speech Acts

Speech acts can be direct, with a clear purpose. For example, if someone says "I won't join you today," it is obvious that the purpose of the speech act is to indicate that the speaker will not accompany the listener. However, speech acts can also be indirect, in which case their purpose is less clear. For example, the above sentence could be changed to "I'm afraid that it would be difficult for me to join you today," which is politer, but less clear. The tone of voice (see chapter B2.1), circumstances in which a speech act is uttered, and how certain phrases are used in the speech act can greatly influence the directness and interpretation. This chapter will explain how to take clues from the surrounding circumstances for situational awareness, introduce hedging techniques that can affect the intention, politeness level, and meaning of a speech act, and examine these elements in four common indirect speech acts: suggestions, requests, refusals, and apologies. In addition, the chapter will explain several hedging techniques that can also affect the intention, politeness level, and meaning of a speech act.

Taking Clues from the Surrounding Circumstances
One of the main reasons that speakers in English use indirect language is politeness. In general, the more indirect an expression is, the politer it is considered to be. However, English does not contain specific verb forms that indicate politeness, like *sonkeigo*, *kenjougo*, and *teineigo* in Japanese. Instead, a variety of indirect expressions can be used in English to mark politeness. Therefore, it is first helpful to understand in what situations English speakers are likely to use indirect expressions for politeness.

Much as in Japanese, in English, a speaker will use polite language with a person who is in a higher power position than them, such as a boss at work or a teacher at a university. One clue that someone considers another to be in such a position is their use of a title before the person's last name (e.g. Mr. Stevens, Ms. Smith, Dr. Johnson, Professor Brown, etc.) or an honorific (e.g. sir, ma'am). In such situations, expect to hear more indirect speech that must be interpreted beyond its literal meaning. English speakers will also tend to be politer when speaking with strangers. A clue that someone does not know another person is if they start an interaction with a polite expression, such as "excuse me" or "pardon," to get the other person's attention. However, they are less likely to use such expressions with schoolmates and other staff members, regardless of their age (i.e. in English culture, there is little to no concept of *senpai* and *kohai*). The biggest clue that two people are not using polite speech with each other is if they use each other's first names without any positions or titles. However, it should be noted that English speakers will use polite indirect speech even with people who are close to them if they must make a difficult request, give bad news or say something that might be unfavorable to the listener.

When interpreting indirect speech, it is also important to consider the context – the connections between what is said and the content of the other parts of the conversation. If the meaning of a phrase is not clear from its literal interpretation, try considering the following questions:

What is the relationship between the speakers?
What does the speaker want the listener to do?
What information do the speaker and the listener(s) share?
What is the speaker's attitude towards the listener or situation?

For example, the phrase "Let's not talk about what happened last week" could mean several things depending on what the speaker did last week or what he or she knows about what happened. However, because the speaker does not want to talk about it, we can probably assume that "what happened last week" was something negative or possibly embarrassing. Unless the conversation continues or the listener has some extra information about the incident, it is not clear why, precisely, the conversation participants should not talk about what happened. However, even without additional knowledge, a listener could perhaps also infer certain points by paying attention to the speaker's tone of voice, facial expressions or clues from the environment. For example, if the speaker seems embarrassed, ashamed, secretive, or angry, we can imagine that the incident was something negative, whereas if they seem lighthearted or simply shy, we can guess that the incident may not have been so serious.

Hedging

Hedging is a language technique that is often used to make a speech act more indirect and therefore politer and more effective. A number of different words can be used for hedging. They can be paired with indirect expressions to soften a statement and make it politer, or they can be used on their own to reduce the strength or certainty with which an idea is proposed. One way this can be done is through the use of modal verbs. Refer to the chart of modal verb strength in Chapter A2.2, and notice how modal verbs can be added to expressions to soften them or changed to make them weaker or less certain.

> I **want** your help tomorrow. (certain)
>
> I **may want** your help tomorrow. (less certain; your help might not be needed)
>
> You **should** study harder for tomorrow's test. (direct, not as polite)
>
> You **may want to** study harder for tomorrow's test. (less direct, politer)

Another common type of hedging involves the use of words that show uncertainty. These can appear as nouns (e.g. possibility), adjectives (e.g. possible), or adverbs (e.g. possibly). Many of these words appear in hedges as various parts of speech, so it is best to remember them as word families (see Chapter A1.2). Below is a chart of words that show uncertainty and examples of them in use. Note that for many examples, a dummy subject (i.e. "it" or "there") is used, which prevents the speaker from being the subject of the sentence, making the statement less direct and therefore politer.

Word (family)	Example
possible, possibly, possibility	There is a possibility that I will join you.
probable, probably, probability	It is probable that global warming affects our lives now.
(un)likely, likelihood	The likelihood of his theory being true is low.
hope, hopeful, hopefully	It is hoped that this discovery will benefit society.
conceivable, conceivably	Conceivably, the results of this study can advance our understanding of physics.
to some degree / extent, somewhat	I think it is an important work, to some extent.
kind of	I kind of want to join your study session.

Finally, word choice can be used to soften or weaken expressions. Specifically, the connotation or strength (see Chapter A2.1) of the verb used in the sentence can change how certain or polite the statement is. The following verbs are generally used in hedging to weaken or soften an expression.

Verb	Example
believe	It is believed to be a valid way of reducing flooding in the area.
seem	It seems that ultraviolet radiation can kill most bacteria.

assume	I assume that he has done enough background research.
suggest	The data suggests that high cholesterol increases the risk of a heart attack.
indicate	Previous studies indicate that drinking water reduces the chance of getting headaches.
appear	It appears that more studying time is correlated with higher grades.
doubt	I doubt that there is enough evidence to say that for sure.
mention	I mentioned that he wanted to participate last week.

It should be noted that more than one hedge can be used in a single expression and further combined with the phrases that indicate indirect speech acts given in the previous section. In general, the more indirect a sentence is and the more hedging it includes, the less certain or politer it seems. Consider the following examples:

Please let me join your laboratory. (direct request, not rude, but not very polite)

I **was hoping you would** let me join your laboratory. (+ indirectness)

I was hoping you **might** let me join your laboratory. (+ weaker modal verb)

I was hoping that you might **possibly** let me join your laboratory. (+ uncertainty)

The final sentence is very polite because it employs an indirect phrase (emphasizing the speaker's feelings), uses a weaker modal verb ("might" instead of "would"), and adds a word that shows uncertainty ("possibly"). Notice that the first sentence is not rude, but it does not use any indirectness or hedging and thus is not very polite either. A similar pattern applies when a speaker or writer attempts to express that they are not entirely sure about something, such as research results, as in the following examples:

Acupuncture **is** an effective method of treating chronic pain.
  (very confident)

Acupuncture **could be** an effective method of treating chronic pain.
  (+ modal verb)

Acupuncture could **possibly** be an effective method of treating chronic pain.
  (+ uncertainty)

It seems that acupuncture could possibly be an effective method of treating chronic pain.
  (+ dummy subject, + weak verb)

The final sentence is more likely to be found in research reports because it usually takes decades of testing and retesting before scientists can agree and be certain of new discoveries. Therefore, even when there is data in support of an idea, scientific papers tend to use some of the hedges, as exemplified above, to varying degrees, depending on how convincing the data is and how much previous research supports the conclusion.

Suggestions

One of the main reasons that speakers in English use indirect language is politeness. In general, the suggestions include giving advice, issuing an invitation, and making a statement of disapproval or criticism. Advice and recommendations are usually positive, whereas disapproval and criticism are negative, but these acts all have the potential to hurt the listener's feelings or irritate them, especially when they did not ask for the suggestion. Therefore, indirectness is often used with suggestions.

Indirect suggestions can be categorized into three basic types: rhetorical questions, giving advice to others, and imaginary suggestions. A rhetorical question is a question to which the speaker does not really expect an answer. Although some are used to simply lament (e.g. "Why does this always happen to me?!") or express surprise (e.g. "He said what?!"), rhetorical questions can also be used to make suggestions, in which case the speaker simply expects the listener to follow the advice rather than necessarily answer the question. Giving advice to others involves making a suggestion in general or directing it to a large group or category of people to which the listener belongs. Though the speaker does not say that the listener, specifically, should follow the advice, they usually expect the listener to realize that they belong to the category being addressed and thus that they should follow the advice. Imaginary suggestions involve using conditional language (e.g. if, when) or the subjunctive mood (e.g. would, could) to talk about a situation or scenario that is not real. For example, in the suggestion "If I were you, I would start exercising," the speaker is not the listener; he or she is imagining that they are the listener and then talking about this hypothetical situation. However, the speaker expects the listener to imagine the situation and realize that this is a suggestion. Below are some typical examples of expressions in these categories.

Type	Expression	Example
rhetorical questions	Why not… / Why don't you…	Why not use the lab manual?
	Have you / Did you…?	Have you tried visiting the student learning center?
giving advice to others or advice in general	should / had better	Students shouldn't cheat on their tests.
	the best way to…	The best way to study for the test is to try the practice test first.
	It could/might be…	It might be a good idea to study harder.
imaginary suggestions	If I were you	I wouldn't do that if I were you.
	You might want to…	You might want to close the door after you leave.

	If you think about it...	If you think about it, there is only one thing you can do.

Requests

Requests include asking for favors, giving orders, and issuing warnings. Though asking for favors is usually done by someone in a lower position, and giving orders and warnings is usually done by someone in a higher position, all of them involve getting someone else to do something that they may not want to do. Therefore, indirectness is often used in these situations.

Indirect requests can be categorized into four basic types: embedded questions, acknowledging the listener's trouble, emphasizing the speaker's feelings, and imaginary requests. Embedded questions are those in which the speaker hides the real request by putting it inside of another question or statement. For example, in the embedded question "Do you know what time it is?," the speaker wants to know what time it is, not whether the listener has this information. An embedded question is usually used to provide the listener with an excuse to not comply with the request (e.g. "I don't know what time it is") and is thus considered politer than a direct question. Acknowledging the listener's trouble occurs when the speaker includes an expression that shows the listener that they understand that they are imposing on the listener. Emphasizing the speaker's feelings is a way of encouraging the listener to act by asking them to consider how the speaker will feel if they accept the request (i.e. positive) or decline it (i.e. negative). Imaginary requests are the same as imaginary suggestions, in that they involve using conditional language (e.g. if, when) or the subjunctive mood (e.g. would, could) to talk about a situation or scenario that is not real. For example, "Would you take me to the station?" may seem like a direct request, but it actually asks the question, "If I asked you to take me to the station (but I am not actually asking), what would you answer?" Below are some typical expressions used to make indirect requests.

Type	Expression	Example
embedded questions	Do you think / know ...	Do you think you could help me?
	I wonder (if)	I wonder who that professor is.
acknowledging the listener's trouble	...too much trouble...	If it's not too much trouble, please help me with my homework.
	I hate to ask but...	I hate to ask, but will you lend me your textbook until next week?
	Can / could...	Can you come by later, or are you busy?
emphasizing the speaker's feelings	It would be nice...	It would be nice if you turned your homework in on time.
	I was hoping...	I was hoping you would help me.
imaginary requests	Would you like to…	Would you like to help me later?

	Would you mind...	Would you mind turning in your report early?

Refusals

Refusals include declining various types of suggestions and requests. Although it is perhaps more difficult to refuse a request than a suggestion, both are rejections of the listener's ideas, and thus indirectness is often used to prevent offending the listener. Indirect refusals can be categorized into three basic types: expressing regret, giving excuses or reasons, and pointing to uncertainty or discomfort. Expressing regret usually involves talking about sorrow or wishing to not have to refuse. Giving excuses or reasons is typically done so that the listener will not blame or be angry with the speaker. Finally, if a speaker answering a request does not directly refuse, but instead seems uncertain of their feelings or their response, or if they simply mention the burden it would cause them, they generally expect the listener to *infer* that they are refusing. This is especially true when tone of voice is used with certain words and phrases, such as "could" or "I don't know" (see Chapter B2.1). Below are some typical expressions used to refuse requests.

Type	Expression	Example
expressing regret	If only...	If only I didn't have class at that time.
	I wish...	I wish I could go, but I have other plans.
giving excuses or reasons	I already...	I already promised my mother I would help her.
	The thing is...	The thing is, I've already made other plans.
	Don't worry about it (reason)	Don't worry about it, I have enough people to help me.
pointing to uncertainty or discomfort	I'm not sure... / I don't know (if)...	I'm not sure if that is a good idea.

Apologies

Apologies can be made for a number of reasons, but they are given when the speaker has done something that they fear might upset the listener or when they have already offended the listener. Therefore, apologies often include some indirect expression to increase politeness. They often but do not always include a word that shows remorse, such as "sorry." Furthermore, even if an expression includes the word "sorry," it is not necessarily an apology. For example, consider the non-apology "I'm sorry that John did that." Although this includes the phrase "I'm sorry," here this phrase only indicates that the speaker feels bad, and the next phrase "that he did that" indicates that the speaker thinks it is John's fault and not their own. Although they are expressing sympathy, they are not taking responsibility for the bad situation and are not apologizing.

Apologies can be categorized into four basic types: acknowledging responsibility, explaining, expressing concern for the listener, and making offers or promises. Acknowledging responsibility means that the speaker is accepting that they did something wrong. Offering explanations is a way to make the listener less angry by either showing that the speaker is not the only one who is wrong or that they did their best in the situation. Expressing concern for the listener means that the speaker says something to show that they understand the listener's feelings and are remorseful. Finally, offers or promises are attempts by the speaker to remedy the situation by doing or promising to do something to either help the listener or ensure the mistake will not happen again. Below are some typical expressions used to make apologies.

Type	Expression	Example
acknowledging responsibility	I'll admit ... (should have)	I'll admit that I should have checked the logbook before consulting you.
	(self-insult)	I can't believe I was so inconsiderate!
	I apologize / my mistake	I apologize, that was my mistake.
explaining	you (can) see...	I tried to help, but you can see I don't have much free time.
	...didn't realize...	Oh, I didn't realize you were busy.
	didn't mean to	Sorry, I didn't mean to! (it was an accident)
expressing concern for the listener	I know (that) ...	I know that you must be angry with me.
making offers or promises	...won't happen again	Don't worry, it won't happen again.
	do you want me (to)...	Do you want me to talk to the professor for you?
	...if you want...	Oops! I can fix it if you want.
	...but I can / will...	I'm so sorry I broke it, but I can get you a new one.
	I'll tell you what... (offer)	I'll tell you what, I will pay for the second half.

Students should also be aware of common expressions in which the speaker refuses to accept blame and thus does not apologize. There are three basic strategies for doing this, which might appear similar to those above but must be differentiated: non-acceptance, justification, and shifting blame. Non-acceptance means that the speaker denies either that the act happened or that they are responsible. For example, if someone says "I'm sorry that you feel that way," this is not an apology. It is an expression of regret that the listener feels bad, but one in which the speaker assigns the blame for the feelings to the listener. Justification involves the speaker giving reasons that they should not be at fault. Justification differs from explanation because with explanation, the speaker accepts some or all of the responsibility but is asking the listener for forgiveness, whereas with justification the speaker does not accept responsibility. Shifting blame is a strategy by which the speaker does not admit that they were wrong and instead suggests someone else should be blamed. Examples of expressions used in each of these strategies are provided below.

Type	Expression	Example
non-acceptance	...not on (me)... / not my fault	Your test score is not on me!
	I would never...	I would never miss a question like that.
justification	...take into consideration... the fact that...	You're not taking into consideration the fact that I only had two days to do the assignment.
	...bound to happen...	With my busy schedule, this was bound to happen.
non-acceptance, passing the blame	What about...	Yes, I am in charge of payments, but what about George, who is in charge of ordering?
	<person> is the one (who)...	You're the one who told me not to come after 11 a.m.

Examples of Speech Acts in Use

Look at the example conversations below and then try to guess the answers. A QR Code linked to a recording of the conversations is provided at the end. Notice that finding the correct answer requires that you understand what speech act is being performed. Many of the speech acts are indirect and exhibit hedging, as indicated by the bold words.

> MAN: **I hate to ask**, but **do you think** you could practice elsewhere?
> WOMAN: Oops, I **didn't mean to** bother you. **How about** the hallway? That **should** be far enough away.

1) What is the woman likely to do next?
   (A) Practice in the hallway
   (B) Help the man move into the hallway
   (C) Continue practicing where she is
   (D) Stop practicing

In this example, the man indirectly requests that the woman practice somewhere else by utilizing both the strategy of thinking about the listener (i.e. "I hate to ask") and an embedded question (i.e. "do you think..."). The woman offers an apology by giving an explanation (i.e. "I didn't mean to bother you") and offers to fix the situation by accepting the man's request and suggesting that she move to the hallway. Since she has not refused his request, "C" is not correct. Furthermore, though she accepts his request, her proposed solution is to practice in the hallway, making "A" the correct choice.

> WOMAN: Oh no! I have to do better on my next test…
>
> MAN: **Why don't you** join my study group?
>
> WOMAN: **I'm not sure** that's a good idea. I tried it earlier in the year, but most of the members **seemed kind of** unserious, and I didn't do well on that test either.
>
> MAN: I'm sorry, but that's **not my fault**. It was **bound to happen** with people like John in the group. He's since left though, so **if I were you**, I'd give it another chance.
>
> WOMAN: Hmmm…**I already** told Jane I'd join her group though…

What can be inferred from the above discussion?
  (A) The man feels responsible of the woman's poor test score
  (B) The woman will probably join the man's study group
  (C) The man needs the woman in his group
  (D) The woman feels the man's study group is not serious enough

In this example, "A" is incorrect because although the man says "I'm sorry," he is not apologizing. Instead, he does not accept responsibility, shifts blame, and gives justification as to why the lack of seriousness in his study group is not his fault. In addition, the man suggests that the woman should join his study group but does not request that she do so, and he does not mention that it would benefit him. Therefore, it is not reasonable to assume that "C" is true. The woman indirectly refuses the man's suggestion twice, first by expressing uncertainty (i.e. "I'm not sure") and then by giving a reason (i.e. she already told Jane she would join her group), so "B" is also incorrect. Finally, though the woman hedges her complaint that the man's study group is not serious (with "seem" and "kind of"), this is only to make the complaint easier for the man to hear, and her real opinion is clearly that the group is unserious. Therefore, "D" is the correct answer.

B2.3 Fluency and Pronunciation

Being able to speak competently about a topic requires a certain degree of fluency and accuracy. Fluency is how long one can speak without pausing or taking breaks in their presentation of ideas. Pronunciation is how words and phrases are spoken and includes both individual sounds and groups of sounds. Pausing too frequently or for too long and having bad pronunciation and intonation will prevent the listener from understanding what the speaker is saying. Therefore, students at Tohoku University require a certain level of fluency and accuracy when discussing research ideas, giving presentations, and conveying the results of their research.

What to Know about Fluency and Pronunciation

The skills of fluency and pronunciation are required for a number of different speaking tasks, including oral reporting, orally summarizing from notes (see Chapter B1.2), giving opinions (see Chapter B1.4), and presenting on topics (see Chapter C4). In order to improve their fluency, students need to know how to monitor their fluency and what to do when they have a breakdown in speech. In order to improve their pronunciation, students must be aware of how to make individual sounds but also of how to properly pronounce groups of words and sounds together.

Monitoring and Improving Fluency
To check their spoken fluency, students can choose a topic and try speaking about it for a set amount of time, such as one or two minutes. If the speech is recorded, students can easily check how long they are able to speak about a topic, and by transcribing their speech, they can see how many words or syllables they used. Although this is not a perfect measurement of fluency, the number of words a student is able to produce about a particular topic in a given amount of time gives an indication of how fluent they are. By attempting this task every few weeks, students can see whether they are improving their oral fluency.

To improve their oral fluency, students can try to memorize the set patterns, expressions, and collocations given in the other chapters in this book (Chapters B1.2, B1.3, B1.4, B2.2, A2.4, etc.). Even if students can recognize the set expressions, practice is needed to be able to use them fluently in speech. Thus, using these set expressions in solitary speaking practice such as that described in the previous paragraph is critical to improving oral reporting skills. Furthermore, improving fluency requires that students develop their ability to speak at length about various topics with little to no preparation. Students can begin to improve this ability by first focusing on speaking as much as possible. In order to do this, students should practice presenting their opinion and thinking of as many supporting details as they can in a short amount of time. For examples of this and expressions that might help, see Chapter B1.3. Once students are able to talk about a topic for the entire set time (i.e. one to two minutes), they should work on speaking more quickly. However, this does not mean saying the words more quickly. Rather, this means using fillers and repeats to naturally fill the pauses in their speech. Simply repeating what one has already said or restarting allows the speaker to continue talking without leaving a long silence that makes the listener wonder whether they have finished. Fillers are words or phrases that help maintain the conversation and signal to the listener that the speaker is not yet finished speaking but is instead thinking of what to say next. Although words such as "uhhh…" or "ummm…" can be used, they are not well respected in academic English, so consider trying some of the following fillers instead.

...the thing is...	…(what) I mean (is)...	well...
what I'm trying to say is...	it turns out that...	let me see...

Consider the following two short oral reports about a topic, one with fillers and repeats and one without. Notice that the one that contains fillers and repeats has fewer pauses and more words, which makes it easier for the listener to follow and understand that the speaker is not yet finished.

I will talk about the school's policy of adding more online classes… in my opinion… it is a good idea… because… because it will make more… classes available to students.

I will talk about the school's policy of adding more online classes. **Let me see. Well,** in my opinion, it is a good idea. **What I'm trying to say is**, it is a good idea because it will make more classes. **The thing is**, more classes means more available classes for students, so I think it is a good idea.

Monitoring and Improving Pronunciation

To check their pronunciation ability, students can try speaking into an automatic speech recognition program, such as the voice input function on a word processing program (e.g. Microsoft Word, Google Docs, etc.) or a smartphone search application. Noticing where the program does and does not transcribe the speech correctly will give students some idea of what words or phrases they are mispronouncing to the extent that others cannot understand them. While this is also not a perfect measurement of pronunciation, aiming to improve the pronunciation of these words and phrases to the point that such programs will recognize them will surely help students improve their overall oral reporting.

To improve their pronunciation, students should make a note of the words and phrases they are mispronouncing and then try to determine what mistakes they are making. Below are some common difficulties that Japanese learners have when learning English pronunciation that students should consider.

1. Individual Sounds

In general, Japanese has fewer sounds than English. Therefore, many Japanese learners of English tend to conflate two different sounds into one sound. For example, there is no "r" or "l" sound in Japanese, so both of these sounds famously sound like the Japanese "r" sound. Below is a chart of many sounds that are often mistakenly conflated into one sound by Japanese learners of English. Students should check the chart and ensure that they can pronounce and hear the difference in these related sounds. Students should be aware that there are some differences in various English dialects. The examples below are given in both British and American pronunciation for reference. Students should listen to a variety of English accents to become familiar with any differences in pronunciation. They can practice correctly making these sounds by speaking them into a voice dictation software.

Mistaken Conflation	Sound 1	Sound 2
ɾ (i.e. ら)	"r" (e.g. "pray")	"l" (e.g. "play")
b	"b" (e.g. "ban")	"v" (e.g. "van")
s	"s" (e.g. "sing")	"th" (e.g. "thing")
shi	"sh" (e.g. "shine")	"s" (e.g. "sign")
z	"z" (e.g. "zen")	"th" (e.g. "then")
あ	"a" (e.g. "hat")	"u" (e.g. "hut")
い	"ee" (e.g. "bean")	"i" (e.g. "bin")
お	"o" (e.g. "not")	"o" (e.g. "note")

2. Phonemic Stress

In most languages, including Japanese, some syllables in a word receive more stress (also referred to as "phonemic stress") than others. In some languages, such as English, the amount of phonemic stress is more noticeable than in others. In English, phonemic stress can result in a change in vowel sound, and some words even have two different phonemic stresses depending on whether they are being used as a verb or a noun. Because this stress can change the meaning of a sentence, it is important to understand the basic concepts related to phonemic stress. Below are some general guidelines.

a. There is only one phonemic stress per word.

b. For two-syllable words, nouns and adjectives are usually stressed on the first syllable, whereas verbs are generally stressed on the second syllable.
   (e.g.) EXport = noun; exPORT = verb
   REcord = noun; reCORD = verb

c. Words ending with the suffixes (see Chapter A1.1) -*ic* and -*tion* usually place stress on the syllable just before the suffix.

      (e.g.) aMORPHic, hisTORic, evaluAtion, conDItion

d. Words ending with the suffixes -*al*, -*y*, and -*ity* usually place stress on the third syllable from the end.

      (e.g.) conSENsual, biOlogy,   inaBILity

3. Linking

Linking is when two separate words are blended together when they are pronounced. Well-known examples include contractions (e.g. "you are" becomes "you're," and "I am" becomes "I'm"), but there are also several instances when linking occurs in pronunciation but not in writing. The four most common examples of this are you-linking, of-linking, common sound linking, and consonant-vowel linking. You-linking occurs when the word "you" appears after a word ending in a consonant, resulting in a blend, similar to the y- blends in Japanese. Consider the following examples.

Blend	Example	Linked Pronunciation
d + you = ju	Would you...	Wouju...
t + you = chu	I know what you...	I know whachu...
n + you = nyu	Can you...	Canyu...

Of-linking is used with the word "of" and results in "of" being blended with the previous word and pronounced as a short "u". Consider the following examples.

a lot of money   → a lott(u) money
out of town   → out(u) town
some of these   → some(u) these

Common sound linking occurs when a word begins with the consonant sound that the previous word ended with. In this case, the words are linked and pronounced as one. This occurs as long as the two consonant sounds are the same, even if the letter used to spell the sound differs across the two words. Consider the following examples.

first time   → firs_time
it's so   → its_o
black coffee   → bla_coffee

Consonant-vowel linking occurs when a one-syllable word that begins with a vowel appears before a word that ends in an unvoiced hard consonant. In American and Canadian English, if the consonant is a "t" sound, it is voiced, causing it to be pronounced like a "d," but this is not generally true for British and Australian English. Consider the following examples:

The plane just took off   → The plane just too_koff.

He looks up to his brother → He loo_ksup to his brother.

I bought it yesterday   → I bou_dit yesterday

4. Reduction

Reduction is when certain sounds are simply not pronounced at all. The following are some of the most common reductions in spoken English.

Reduction	Example
he, him, her → 'e, 'im, 'er	What did he want? → What did 'e want?
going to → gonna	I'm going to visit Australia. → I'm gonna visit Australia.
have to → hafta	I have to go now. → I hafta go now.
has to → hasta	He has to get a job. → He hasta get a job.
give me → gimme	Give me three of those. → Gimme three of those.
and → 'n	I like salt and pepper. → I like salt 'n pepper.
are → 're	Mom and Dad are coming. → Mom and Dad're coming.

5. Rhythm and Stress

In stress-based languages such as English, the duration of an utterance's pronunciation depends on the number of stressed syllables it contains. Generally, content words (nouns, pronouns, verbs, adjectives, and adverbs) are stressed or contain at least one stressed syllable, whereas function words (those that have grammatical significance but carry little meaning, such as auxiliary verbs and grammatical prepositions) are unstressed. Consider the following sentence. Note that more stress is placed on the content words, in bold, which are therefore longer in duration than the function words.

(e.g.) **Help Mike carry** all of the **boxes** to the **attic.**

In general, unstressed syllables will be spoken more quickly than stressed syllables in order to maintain a basic number of stressed syllables per second, which creates rhythm. Therefore, even if the number of syllables in a sentence increases, the amount of time needed to produce the sentence remains roughly the same, unless new content words are introduced. Other syllables are either linked, reduced, or pronounced more quickly in order to maintain the time needed to produce the sentence. Consider the following example sentences, which get progressively longer but contain the same number of content words. They will all be pronounced in the same amount of time.

> **Dogs hate cats**.
> My **dogs hate cats**.   → (my) dogs hate cats.
> My **dogs hate** your **cats**.   → (my) dogs hacher cats.
> My **dogs** will **hate** your **cats**. → (my) dogs'll hacher cats.
> My **dogs** are going to **hate** your **cats**. (my) dogs'r gonna hacher cats.

In the examples above, the stressed and unstressed syllables create a rhythm, similar to that of music. The stressed syllables are like whole notes, whereas the unstressed syllables are like half or quarter notes that are compressed to fit within the same amount of time. In other words, although the number of syllables in each of the phrases differs, the number of beats needed to say them remains the same. Keeping this in mind and finding the rhythm of the English language can help students' pronunciation to sound more natural.

Example of Fluency and Pronunciation in Use

Use the QR code at the end of this chapter to listen to examples of the pronunciation points above and the two example answers to the question "What is an appropriate amount of sleep for a university student to get each night?" Notice that the first example contains few fillers and repeats and does not make use of stress and rhythm, whereas the second example does. Students should aim to speak more like the second example. Scripts of these examples are provided below.

Example 1
An appropriate amount... of sleep for... university students... is about six hours... each night because... it is healthiest.

Example 2
An appropriate amount(u) sleep for university students_is, well, about six hours. It_turns_out that six hours(u) sleep_is good because, the thing_is, it_is very healthy for students. What_I mean_is that anything less than six hours_is unhealthy.

B2.4 Discussion Strategies

Discussing academic topics involves asking questions, getting information, and exchanging ideas about study or research related topics. Students at Tohoku University must engage in discussions when studying with other students, checking their information with teachers and peers, deciding how to proceed with research, and giving academic presentations. Therefore, students must work to develop discussion strategies that will help them to successfully obtain information and exchange ideas efficiently with others.

What to Know about Discussion Strategies

Having a discussion is different from having a casual conversation because there is usually some purpose to a discussion. Generally, an academic discussion requires that all participants give their ideas and opinions and compare these to those of others. A discussion usually ends when a decision has been reached or all parties have received all of the information that they wanted from the other participants. In order to have a fruitful discussion, students must be able to use and recognize a variety of greetings, elicit responses from others, and give information themselves. Some of these skills have been partially covered in previous chapters. For example, question–response from Chapter B1.3 will be useful for asking questions and giving opinions, and orally summarizing from Chapter B1.2 can help for giving detailed information to others. Therefore, this chapter focuses on greetings, how to elicit responses from others, and useful phrases for discussions.

Greetings

Opening greetings, which are simple greetings between speakers at the beginning of a conversation, are an important part of a discussion. Responding fluently to unfamiliar opening greetings allows the discussion to begin smoothly. Incorrectly responding or not responding at all can cause the dialogue to break down altogether and result in embarrassment for both the greeter and the listener.

There are many opening greetings in English, but most belong to one of two types. Roughly 70% of English opening greetings consist of "one turn" between speakers (e.g. "How are you?" "I'm fine, thanks."), and approximately 20% consist of "one-and-a-half turns" between speakers, such as "How are you?" "I'm fine, thanks. And you?" Despite their simplicity, there are many different words that can be used in standard greetings, so learners may not always recognize what someone says as a simple greeting. However, there are two basic patterns of greetings: those that start with "how" and those that start with "what". Learning to recognize these and some of the sample responses below can help make them easier to understand and respond to, even if slightly different patterns or vocabulary are used.

Common HOW Greetings		
How are you?	How's everything?	How's life?
How's school?	How's it going?	How are you doing?

Although the above phrases seem to be asking complex questions, they are often used in place of a simple "hello," and the asker generally does not expect a lengthy answer. Therefore, similar basic responses can be used for all of them. However, because they ask the question "how," it is inappropriate to respond with words such as "hello" or "yes." To respond to such greetings, it is common to use a positive adjective such as "fine," "good," "great," "pretty good," or "fantastic." These greetings can be followed by asking a similar question or returning the same question to the asker (e.g. "And you?").

Common WHAT Greetings		
What's going on?	What's happening?	What's up?
What's new?	What've you been up to?	What'd you do today?

Although technically there are a wide variety of available responses to the above questions, roughly 80% of opening "what"-greetings consist of one turn or one-and-a-half turns between speakers. As such, though the listener can add more information if they want to, the most common responses are "not too much," "nothing," and "nothing much…" The question can then be returned to the asker (e.g. "And you?") or a similar question can be asked. Similar to the "how"-greetings, these questions are generally recognized as basic greetings, and it is considered strange to answer them too directly or with too much personal information. Furthermore, it is important to note that these greetings cannot be answered with a simple "hello" or a positive adjective such as "good."

Eliciting Responses from Others

In order to have an effective discussion, input is needed from all participants, whether the discussion is taking place between two people or within a small group. However, regardless of the number of participants, sometimes one member does not contribute as much to the discussion as the other(s) or fails to provide adequate responses. There are several reasons that this might occur: they might lack confidence in their speaking ability, awareness that their response was insufficient, or knowledge of how else they can add to the conversation. The responsibility to keep the conversation going does not lie with any single participant, so when lapses in the discussion occur, it is important to be ready to elicit responses from another participant. This can be done in a number of ways.

If a participant simply has not answered a question, it can be asked again, but it should probably be rephrased in a way that makes it easier to understand. If this does not work, the asker can try to guess what the listener's answer might be and seek confirmation (e.g. "Maybe you disagree, is that right?"). However, if the participant answers a question but does not give an expected answer, a follow-up question or statement can be used. Below are some common ones:

What do you mean (by that)?	What are you saying?
Can you give me more details?	Are you saying that ....?
Can you be more specific?	I can't understand why/how....?

If a participant has not been asked a question but has simply failed to respond to a statement, adding a simple question that asks for confirmation can be a good way to elicit a response, which will let the original speaker know if the other participant has understood and agrees with what has been said. Below are some common questions for doing this:

Does that make sense?   Do you see what I'm saying?   Do you know what I mean?

Leading a Group Discussion

When several people participate in a discussion together, it can become difficult to share ideas because some people might not know when to take turns speaking. One way to ensure that everyone in a group has a chance to speak and does not interrupt or distract from others is to decide on a discussion leader. It is the job of the leader to then: introduce the purpose, ask for opinions, elicit responses from the members, react to statements, summarize the opinions, and direct the discussion to new topics. Many of the phrases related to speech acts and hedging (Chapter B2.2) and giving opinions and using interrogatives (Chapter B1.3) will be useful for asking for opinions, and many of the phrases in Chapter B2.2 will be helpful when summarizing. However, a leader must also guide and maintain academic conversations by introducing the purpose, expressing surprise or reacting to a statement, directing the discussion, and ending a topic or the entire discussion. Below is a list of other words and phrases that will be useful for doing so.

For Introducing the Purpose of a Discussion		
Today, we need to...	The reason we're meeting is...	Let's begin by...
For Expressing Surprise or Reacting to a Statement		
Really?!	You're kidding!	Oh no! / Oh, right!
That's an interesting point.	I see what you mean.	That makes sense.

For Directing the Discussion		
Getting back to the point...	Anyway...	By the way...
Let's move on.	Wait (just) a minute.	What about...?
So...	I was gonna say...	Well...
For Ending a Topic or the Entire Discussion		
So we all agree that...	Alright then...	I'm gonna go.
If there are no other ideas...	Why don't we stop for today?	We should end here.

Finally, it is important to remember that when having a group discussion, as opposed to when speaking with only one other person, it is not always clear who the leader is talking to. Therefore, it will be important to remember to use group members' names with most of the above phrases. For example, if a group leader simply says "are there any ideas?" or "what do you think?" it is unclear who should speak, and so the other members will likely hesitate, causing the conversation to break down. Instead, consider saying things such as "do you have any ideas, John?" or "what do you think, Stacey?" as these expressions make it clear who should speak next, preventing confusion and maintaining the conversation.

Examples of Discussion Strategies in Use

Listen to the sample discussions linked in the QR code at the end of this chapter and look at the scripts provided below. Notice how they both start with typical greeting phrases and also makes great use of the question–response patterns mentioned in Chapter B1.3. Furthermore, note that during Discussion Number 1, Nick does not always give adequate responses, so Jessica pushes him for more information. Also, pay attention to how Stacey, the unofficial group leader in Discussion Number 2, maintains the conversation by guiding it, changing topics when appropriate, and making sure that everyone gets a chance to give their ideas. Because of her efforts, everyone seems to know whose turn it is to speak. Finally, be aware of the many useful phrases for discussions that can be found throughout the discussions, which have been <u>underlined</u> in the scripts.

Conversation 1: Two Person Discussion

JESSICA: Nick, what's up?

NICK: Oh, nothing much, you?

JESSICA: The same. <u>So</u>, did you do the homework for Professor Anderson's class yet?

NICK: Yeah.

JESSICA: <u>Well</u>, I was wondering if you wanted to compare answers. I thought number 5 was really difficult.

NICK: I guess so.

JESSICA: What do you mean?

NICK: It wasn't so bad. I mean, I finished.

JESSICA: Yeah, but just because you finished doesn't mean it was easy. Do you know what I mean?

NICK: Well, I thought some of the problems were difficult, like Number 1. At first I thought it was easy, but then I realized we also had to calculate the amount of friction.

JESSICA: But what about number 5?

NICK: Oh, right! I don't think that one was so bad. It was pretty straightforward.

JESSICA: I can't understand why you think it was straightforward.

NICK: Really?! Professor Anderson did a similar problem on the board at the end of class.

JESSICA: That makes sense... I had to leave early for a doctor's appointment. Do you think you could show me how to solve it?

NICK: No problem! Why don't we meet at the library later?

Conversation 2: Group Discussion

STACEY: Hi everyone, how's everything?

JASON: Alright.

MARY: I can't complain.

STACEY: Okay, the reason we're meeting is to decide how to use the extra funds left over from the budget. Jason, do you have any ideas?

JASON: Why don't we buy an extra camera? We could really use a second one, and there's no telling when the first one will break.

STACEY: That makes sense. How about you Mary, do you have any ideas?

MARY: I think we should just return the money to the university.

STACEY: Really?! What are you saying?

MARY: Well, we're not supposed to use money from the budget unless it is absolutely necessary for club activities and there is a penalty for using them inappropriately.

STACEY: Are you saying that you think buying a second camera is an inappropriate use of the funds?

MARY: Actually, I don't think it's inappropriate, but what if the university thinks it is? Can we really justify buying another camera when the first one works just fine?

STACEY: I see what you mean. Jason, do you think we can make a good enough argument to buy a second camera?

JASON: That's no problem! The official university rules say that a club can purchase up to three cameras, and we currently only have one. Also, having a second one will allow us to edit the video, which is important for our club activities. Several other clubs have multiple cameras and they haven't received any penalties.

MARY: <u>Really?!</u> Well… if you don't think we'll get in any trouble for it, I am not against buying a second camera.

STACEY: <u>So we all agree that</u> getting a second camera is a good use of the funds. <u>If there are no other ideas</u>, <u>why don't we stop for today</u>?

JASON: Sounds good to me!

English C

Integrated Writing and Presentation

Objective 1: Acquire the ability to write an academic essay

C1 Essay Writing
C2 Citing and Referencing

Objective 2: Acquire the ability to create and give academic presentation

C3 Presentation Preparation
C4 Presentation Strategies

C1 Essay Writing

Essays are short pieces of writing that follow the fundamental Introduction–Body–Conclusion (IBC) format on which most English writing is based. In order to become a good writer of various academic materials, such as lab reports and research papers, students must first master the IBC format in essays. This skill will be especially important at Tohoku University because students will often be required to write final reports for classes, lab reports, and short research papers for their classes or research projects.

What to Know about Essay Writing

Students must be aware what information is expected in each of the three sections. Furthermore, they should be aware that IBC-format essays typically discuss three points and are taught as five-paragraph essays. One paragraph is usually dedicated to the introduction, one to the conclusion, and three to the body, with one main point being discussed per body paragraph.

The Introduction

The introduction is the first paragraph of an essay or the first section of a longer piece of writing. Importantly, introduction paragraphs in essays do not follow the same pattern as most other independent paragraphs, as introduced in Chapter A2.3. Instead, they often begin with a general statement, question, or interesting fact that is designed to catch the reader's attention. An introduction paragraph must then inform the reader of the purpose of the essay as briefly as possible, while providing enough information that this purpose can be understood. Therefore, it is common for introductory paragraphs to describe the current situation, highlight any controversies, and define any key terms directly after the first sentence. The final sentence of an introduction is called the thesis statement: a sentence that clearly states the purpose of the paper or what exactly it is about and provides a short outline of the main points of the body paragraphs. These points are shown below in both a good and a bad example:

Good Example

Most people have probably noticed that the weather is getting increasingly hotter these days, and that it is beginning to cause problems all over the world. Though there are a number of problems facing humanity, the one that threatens life on Earth the most is probably climate change. Climate change refers to the global trend of the planet becoming warmer as well as the various local and global weather patterns that are changing because of this warming. While all nations should be united in fighting climate change, there is a lot of pushback from both individuals and entire countries who claim that climate change is not such a serious issue or that there is nothing that we can do about it. However, I do not accept this premise. I believe there are things that we can and should do to combat climate change, specifically: reduce consumption, increase renewable energy production, and fund climate research.

Bad Example

Do you like using air conditioning? Climate change is a big problem in the world right now. Therefore, I think we should fight climate change. I have three reasons.

Notice that the good example introduction starts with a general statement that is still related to the thesis. In the bad example, the first sentence asks a question, but it is not clear how this relates to the thesis or topic. Next, the good example explains the current situation, which helps the reader to understand why the topic is important and defines the important term "climate change." The bad example transitions from the first sentence to the thesis but does not indicate why the topic is important, nor does it define the key ideas so that the reader can understand the thesis. Finally, notice that the thesis statement in the good example clearly states the purpose of the paper (that we should talk about the issue and change our actions) and outlines the three main points of the paper (the three specific actions that we should take to fight climate change), which we can expect to read about in detail in the body paragraphs. On the other hand, the bad example explicitly states the general topic of the essay (stopping climate change), but it does not outline what points will appear in the paper. In longer works, such as research papers and lab reports, the introduction may only state the purpose of the text and not outline what is written in later paragraphs or sections. However, statements like "I have three reasons" should never appear – if the introduction mentions that there are three reasons, they must be given!

The Body

Body paragraphs can be found after the introduction. Longer pieces of writing, such as lab reports, research papers, and books, may have several body paragraphs divided across sections. However, standard essays generally have three body paragraphs, one for each of the essay's main points. These paragraphs should follow the basic structure of a paragraph, as introduced in Chapter A2.3. This means that the first sentence of each body paragraph should start with a topic sentence, which introduces the main idea of the paragraph. For essays written in the IBC format, each topic sentence should be one of the three main points outlined in the thesis statement of the introduction. Then, evidence and details should be provided for each topic sentence. For an overview of how to do this, please see Chapter A2.3. Finally, when essays are written in the IBC format, the final sentence in a body paragraph can either be a concluding sentence, which completes an idea, or a transition sentence, which leads to the next main point.

Instead of three body paragraphs, longer works often have three sections, each of which contains multiple paragraphs. For example, most research papers contain five sections: Introduction,

Previous Studies, Methods, Results, and Conclusion. Notice that this pattern follows the basic IBC style, but simply replaces body paragraphs with body sections. Therefore, by learning to recognize and implement the IBC format in an essay, students will be easily able to develop their writing into longer works.

The Conclusion

The conclusion is the final piece of the IBC format and is generally limited to a single paragraph regardless of the length of the work. A good concluding paragraph should begin by restating the purpose or thesis of the paper. Then, it should revisit each of the main points and any relevant information that helps to show why these main points support the thesis or purpose of the essay. Finally, most conclusions end by offering an implication of the points, a connection to the reader, or the writer's ideas for the future. For example, in most research papers, the end of the conclusion makes suggestions for future research or suggests actions to be taken based on the results. These points are shown below in both a good and a bad example:

Good Example

Based on the evidence presented above, I believe that we should reduce consumption, increase renewable energy production, and fund climate research in order to fight global warming. As mentioned above, a reduction in consumption means a reduction in production, which will decrease energy use and fossil fuel use in the transportation of goods. Furthermore, though it is currently not possible to get all of our energy from renewable sources, it is important to increase renewable energy production to encourage more research into these technologies in the future. Finally, funding climate change research is the only way that we will be able to monitor our progress, and it may help us to find new solutions in the future. In conclusion, though it may seem that there is little that any of us can do to make an impact on the whole world, if we all take minor actions, such as those suggested in this paper, we can make significant progress in fixing the problem of climate change.

Bad Example

In conclusion, we should fight climate change. Maybe it is hard for many people to take action, but we can all do little things. If we all make small changes to our lives, we can solve a lot of problems, such as trash production, global warming, and international communication. Therefore, we must fight now!

Notice that the good example repeats the thesis statement using different words and makes sure to include the three main points and the purpose of the paper. The bad example gives the purpose of the paper and includes the words "in conclusion" but fails to outline the paper's three main points. Furthermore, the good example revisits the most significant details related to each main point, whereas the bad example does not. Finally, the good example suggests future action that is based on the paper and connected to the ideas it presents. While the bad example also makes a suggestion (we must fight now), the suggestion is vague, because it is not connected to any of the ideas in the paper. It leaves the reader wondering what the author suggests fighting and how. The bad example makes this especially unclear because it also mentions unrelated topics in the third sentence (i.e. trash production and international communication).

Example of Essay Writing in Use

Look at the sample essay below. Important features of the IBC format in essay writing are emphasized by means of <u>underlining</u> and are then explained in (parentheses).

<u>If you have ever thought about your health, then you are probably aware of the adverse effects that smoking has on your body.</u> **(general statement that catches attention)** Though smoking various substances is common in traditional cultures around the world, modern tobacco products are not part of any specific heritage and are very harmful. In fact, smoking is one of the leading causes of preventable death in the world. While some might think that we should simply outlaw tobacco, this is impossible to do overnight because of its addictive properties and the number of people that smoke. <u>However, I think that we can take measures to stop people from smoking, such as implementing plain packaging of tobacco products, disallowing tobacco advertisements, and increasing vendors' responsibility for tobacco sales.</u> **(thesis statement)**

<u>One way that we can reduce the number of smokers is to enforce plain packaging laws for cigarettes.</u> **(topic sentence; see Chapter A2.3)** Plain packaging laws control the color, text, and graphics of cigarette packages. In general, they disallow the use of branding, logos, and appealing colors or pictures and also require that particular warnings and graphics be printed at certain locations and in certain sizes on the package. These regulations reduce the allure of smoking by preventing marketing tactics from swaying smokers' decisions and also by making warnings more visible. Some people may not think this is enough to hinder tobacco use. However, such laws were implemented in Australia in 2011, and a follow-up study in 2016 confirmed that these changes had caused a dramatic decrease in the number of smokers in the country. Furthermore, plain packaging laws impact society over time, which allows ample opportunity for tobacco manufacturers and smokers to adjust their behavior so that the economy does not have to suffer and people do not have to attempt to quit smoking overnight. <u>When attempting to make societal changes, it is important to give people time to adapt, which is why not only implementing plain packaging but also disallowing tobacco advertising in general is a good idea.</u> **(transition sentence; see Chapter A2.3)**

<u>Disallowing the advertising of tobacco products is another way to discourage</u>

smoking without forcing sudden changes on people. **(topic sentence)** It goes without saying that advertising is a powerful tool that companies use to convince people to buy their products. In general, there are two kinds of advertising: that which seeks to increase customer numbers by having people buy one brand as opposed to another brand, and that which seeks to convince people who do not normally use a product to begin using it. Specifically, the latter type of advertising is problematic when it comes to tobacco. Though there is perhaps no problem with convincing smokers to use a different brand of cigarettes, advertising that attempts to get non-smokers to begin smoking goes against what society is trying to accomplish: improving public health by abolishing smoking. This solution has also proven its worth in a number of countries such as America and Canada, which have seen large decreases in the number of new smokers. Though this may seem like an obvious solution, there are actually still many advertisements for tobacco products around town that are seen by impressionable children and teenagers. Therefore, we should push for similar laws and regulations here. **(concluding sentence; see Chapter A2.3)**

Finally, if we truly wish to reduce the number of smokers, it is imperative that we make vendors responsible for tobacco sales. **(topic sentence)** Specifically, this means that retailers should be punished if they sell cigarettes to young people, who are prohibited from buying them. People often become life-long smokers because of how addictive cigarettes are. Therefore, if we wish to reduce the number of smokers, we must prevent young people from trying them in the first place. That is why our laws currently forbid people under the age of 20 from purchasing tobacco. However, laws without enforcement are meaningless. Because it is too difficult to track down every young person who breaks the law in this way, we should instead place the responsibility on the sellers by requiring them to check for identification and fining them when their failure to do so results in a sale to a minor. Police can check that retailers are complying quite easily, and such efforts have proven effective in countries such as Belgium, France, and New Zealand. Currently, convenience stores ask customers to push a button to confirm that they are 20 years old but do nothing to actually verify this. However, if they feared a heavy fine or other legal action, they would surely take additional measures to ensure that they were not selling cigarettes illegally. By making vendors responsible for sales in this way, they would work with society at large to help prevent underage people from becoming smokers in the first place. **(concluding sentence)**

In summary, it is my belief that we should implement plain packaging laws, abolish advertising, and increase vendor responsibility in order to reduce smoking. **(restatement of the thesis)** For one, plain packaging laws have worked in other countries to decrease the number of smokers by decreasing the appeal of cigarettes. These laws act gradually, which prevents the negative effects of sudden change. Abolishing tobacco advertisements also slowly changes behavior in society by preventing non-smokers from starting to smoke in the first place. Finally, putting more responsibility on tobacco retailers to ensure that cigarettes are not sold to minors can help to reduce the number of new smokers by stopping young people from trying cigarettes. Though these changes may seem extreme to some people, nothing that I have argued for is new, as all these measures have been implemented successfully in other countries. <u>Therefore, I think they are worth trying, as reducing the number of needless deaths by getting rid of cigarettes is an important endeavor for all of humanity.</u> **(implication, connection to the reader or suggestion for future action)**

C2 Citing and Referencing

Citing and referencing are ways in which authors and researchers give credit to other people's ideas and words that they use in their work. Students must also cite and reference other people's unique ideas, theories, information, data, and intellectual property in their work. Citing and referencing, however, is not necessary when making a statement that is common knowledge, such as "The Earth is round." Failing to cite and reference properly can lead to plagiarism, which is stealing someone else's ideas and words and presenting them as your own. Plagiarism is a serious breach (breaking of a rule) of academic honesty that can result in a student's work being failed by instructors or rejected by publishing companies. It can also lead to a ban on presenting at conferences, forfeits (losses) of research funding, and suspension or even expulsion from the university. Citing sources and referencing them correctly is the only way to introduce ideas, words, data, evidence, and any other material that is not exclusively your own. This allows others to verify the facts being reported to ensure the credibility of the work. Therefore, learning to cite and reference correctly is very important for students at Tohoku University, as they must often give credit to other researchers when writing papers and presenting research findings.

What to Know about Citing and Referencing

Students should be aware of how to check for the quality of a source, and how to cite and reference properly. There are several different styles of citing and referencing, which vary depending on the field of study and the preferences of particular teachers, journals, and academic societies. However, the three most popular are the American Psychological Association (APA) (often used in education, psychology, and the sciences), Modern Language Association (MLA) (often used in the humanities), and Chicago (often used in business, history, and fine arts) styles. Though there are many differences between these styles, this chapter will cover many of the common points. When preparing a paper for a class, journal, or academic society, be sure to check the style sheet and guidelines carefully, as there are often special instructions for punctuation and formatting.

Determining the Quality of a Source

Use of questionable sources in a paper can lead to the author accidentally making untrue statements, the reader questioning the author's work, or the paper being poorly reviewed. Therefore, it is important to consider if a source is reliable or trustworthy before citing it in a paper. There are three basic ways to determine if it is acceptable to include a source in a paper: checking the author, checking the date, and cross-referencing.

When considering whether to cite a source, the first consideration should be the author.

Uncertainty regarding who the author is a major concern because it makes it impossible to confirm if the author is an expert in the field. This is why most websites are usually bad sources. Anyone can write a website without the information being verified. Unreferenced websites therefore make it easy for the authors to hide their identities, present inaccurate analyses, and even tell lies. However, if the specific author is unknown because the source was created by a well-known and generally trusted organization, for instance NHK, it can probably be considered trustworthy. If the author is identifiable, it is still important to consider whether they have any biases, conflicts of interest, or motivation to hide the truth. For example, using a company's website to get basic information about when the company was founded or what products they provide is not a problem, but it is not a reliable source of data about the company's potential environmental pollution. If the company is doing something bad, they are motivated to hide the facts. Even if a company were to publish a report on their website about their own bad actions, they would be likely to write the report in a biased way and not to provide all the facts.

The next consideration when choosing a source is the date. While some information and facts do not change over time, other information is very time sensitive, and new data sometimes causes society to change its understanding of the world. For example, if a researcher wants to write about how Japanese people view Russia, it would be unacceptable to cite a paper from 1924 to represent current views because public opinion has probably changed vastly between 1924 and now. The opinions of scientists and experts often change based on new data. For example, researchers in the early 1900s used to believe that humans used only 10% of their brains, but after better equipment was developed, they realized that this was not true. Therefore, it would be dangerous to cite most brain science studies published before 1950.

Finally, cross-referencing can help students and researchers to verify that a source is credible. Cross-referencing means to check what many different sources report about the same information. If the majority of sources seem to agree on a given fact, piece of data, or idea, then it is probably safe to cite that particular information from the source. If most other sources contradict the original source, it is important to think about why this is so, which would probably involve considering the author and date (as suggested above). If there is no consensus among the sources about a particular fact or data set, then there might simply not be enough evidence to verify or disprove it. In that case, it is a good idea to cite multiple sources and suggest that no conclusion has been reached regarding that information.

Citations

An in-text citation is when an author gives credit for an idea in the middle of their writing, usually by providing the name of the person or organization the information came from and the year that it was published or stated. This can be done through direct quotation, when the author's exact words are used, or through indirect quotation, when the author's information or ideas are used but are paraphrased or summarized. Though it is easy to use direct quotations because no paraphrasing is required, authors must be careful not to use too many in a single paper or book. When an author overuses direct quotations, they give very little input of their own, which may lead the reader to question the author's writing ability and can result in publishers rejecting the work. Therefore, only use direct quotations if doing so adds to the argument in the paper or if the quotation is very well known and rely primarily on indirect quotations. Refer to Chapter A1.4 for advice on how to write good summaries and paraphrases when quoting indirectly.

Whether writing a direct or an indirect quotation, the author's surname (family name) and the year of publication can be included either as part of the sentence or at the end of the sentence in parentheses, separated by a comma. If the author's surname is included in the sentence, only the year of publication is contained within the parentheses. For example, if giving an indirect quotation from a paper written in 2017 by someone with the surname "O'Leary," it should appear in one of the following two ways:

1. According to a study by O'Leary (2017), 55% of university students in the UK did not know how to correctly write citations.
2. Many students do not know how to correctly write citations in their academic papers, including 55% of UK university students (O'Leary, 2017).

When using a direct quotation, the words that are the original author's must be enclosed in quotation marks, and the first word in the sentence should be capitalized. Never forget to use quotation marks with a direct quote because quoting directly without using quotation marks is plagiarism! Furthermore, when using a direct quotation, the page number on which the quote can be found must also be included. This is not the case for indirect quotations. If the author's surname is used in the sentence, the page number should appear in parentheses at the end of the sentence, preceded by "p." If the author's surname and date are cited together in parentheses at the end of the sentence, add the page number after the date, preceded by a comma. For example, if someone with the surname "Coyle" wrote the sentence "CLIL is a dual-focused educational approach in which an additional language is used for the learning and teaching of both content and language" on page 1 of a book published in 2010, a direct quote could be given in one of the following two ways:

1. Coyle (2010) states that "CLIL is a dual-focused educational approach in which an additional language is used for the learning and teaching of both content and language" (p.1).
2. CLIL has been described by many scholars, but the most cited definition is that "CLIL is a dual-focused educational approach in which an additional language is used for the learning and teaching of both content and language" (Coyle, 2010, p.1).

If a work has multiple authors, no specified single author, or other special considerations, some other rules apply. When a work has two authors, their surnames should be separated by the word "and" in the text or by an ampersand ("&") in parentheses. When a work has three or more authors, the surname of the first author is given, followed by "et al." Most publications request that when there are between three and five authors, all surnames are given for the first citation in the paper, but when there are six or more authors, the first citation uses the "et al." pattern as well. If the work has no specific author, use the name of the organization or institution that published the report. Many websites and reports include author information, but it is not always easy to find. If the author information is available, use that. If a work has no specific publication date, the abbreviation n.d. (short for "no date") can be used. For websites with no page numbers, the paragraph where the information was found can be used with the abbreviation "para." instead of "p." Finally, if quoting multiple sources who all agree on some piece of information, list the sources in alphabetical order according to the first author's surname. If the citations are given in parentheses, separate the works with a semicolon (";"). Check the examples below for the proper way to handle each of these situations, both outside of and within parentheses.

Two Authors:

Coyle and Hood (2010) stated that "CLIL is a dual-focused educational approach in which an additional language is used for the learning and teaching of both content and language" (p.1).
The most common definition of CLIL states that "CLIL is a dual-focused educational approach in which an additional language is used for the learning and teaching of both content and language" (Coyle & Hood, 2010, p.1).

Multiple Authors:

Johnson et al. (2014) found that the number of greenhouse gases in the air increased by 20% in 2012.
The number of greenhouse gases in the air increased by 20% in 2012 (Johnson et al., 2014).

No Specified Single Author:

According to the Ministry of Justice (2019), the number of foreign residents in Japan is increasing every year.
The number of foreign residents in Japan is increasing every year (Ministry of Justice, 2019).

No Date Given:

Fitzgerald (n.d.) states that zinc oxide is used as an additive in multiple materials because of its high electron mobility.

It has been suggested that zinc oxide is used as an additive in multiple materials because of its high electron mobility (Fitzgerald, n.d.).

No Page Numbers Available:

Kerry (2005) suggests that "Sumeria was the first civilization to produce calendars that have been verified by historians" (para. 7).

It is often suggested that "Sumeria was the first civilization to produce calendars that have been verified by historians" (Kerry, 2005, para. 7).

Citing Multiple Sources for the Same Idea or Piece of Information:

Brown (2005), Johnson and Smith (2012), and Lindenberg et al. (2018) all attest that a good mastery of critical thinking skills correlates with better success in the job market. A good mastery of critical thinking skills is widely believed to correlate with better success in the job market (Brown, 2005; Johnson & Smith, 2012; Lindenberg et al., 2018).

Reporting Verbs

Reporting verbs are necessary to give in-text citations in papers and presentations. As mentioned in Chapter A1.2, using a variety of vocabulary is necessary in academic English, so knowing a number of different verbs for reporting is helpful when writing a paper. Though the denotations of these verbs are similar, the connotations (see Chapter A2.1) and way in which they are used grammatically can be different. Study the chart and examples of common ways of using these verbs below.

Reporting Verbs Indicating the Source Feels Negatively Towards the Idea or Information			
blame	criticize	deny	disparage
doubt	fault	object	question
ridicule	single out		
Reporting Verbs Indicating the Author Does Not Completely Believe the Source			
allege	assume	claim	hypothesize
imply	indicate	infer	suggest

Reporting Verbs with Neutral Connotations			
argue	characterize	consider	decide
define	depict	determine	explain
find	illuminate	indicate	interpret
note	observe	point out	portray
say	state	think	view
Reporting Verbs Indicating the Author Trusts the Source			
acknowledge	admit	conclude	demonstrate
discover	emphasize	observe	reveal
show			
Reporting Verbs Indicating the Source Feels Positively Towards the Idea or Information			
agree	applaud	assert	believe
praise			

Reporting verb + that + <sentence>

Kennedy (2014) argues that most researchers of linguistic relativity have not shown enough evidence for their conclusions.

Fagan (1999) concludes that the data in those studies were both lacking in empirical evidence and theoretically unsound.

Keane (1974) demonstrated that the findings in the national polls were misinterpreted.

The Pathways to English booklet (2019) clearly states that "You should first become familiar with commonly used words and phrases in order to be able to read, write and present data reports" (p.69).

Reporting verb + <person / idea> + for + <noun phrase / gerund>

The work of McGrath (2019) has been praised throughout academia for its innovative research methods (Doyle, 2020).

The findings of Hutton (1982) have been disparaged for their use of unethical research methods (O'Sullivan, 1992).

The Brown and Levinson theory has been criticized for not being applicable to Asian cultures (Murphy, 1991).

Reporting verb + <person / idea> + as <noun phrase / gerund / adjective>

The work of McGrath (2019) has been praised throughout academia as an example of excellence in research methodology (Doyle, 2020).

The Brown and Levinson theory has been criticized as not being applicable to Asian cultures (Murphy, 1991).

The findings of Smith and Johnson (2017) are <u>perceived</u> <u>as</u> <u>conclusive</u> and <u>indisputable</u>.

Referencing

All citations must be included in a "references" section at the end of the paper, which is a list of all of the works cited in the paper that provides more details than are given in the text. The references should be listed in alphabetical order according to the first author's surname. If citing multiple works by the same author or group of authors, order those works by date, from oldest to newest. Finally, the list is usually created with a hanging indent (with the second line further to the right) or with an empty line between each referenced source.

The order of the information and what is included will depend on the style. However, it is common to include the surnames of all authors, the title of the work, the date of publication, and other information related to where the source was published. For example, most referencing styles require that book references include the name of the publisher and the location where the book was published. In general, for articles in newspapers, magazines, and academic journals, authors are required to provide the name of the publication, the volume, the issue, and the page numbers. For book chapters, the name of the book must be given, as well as the chapter name, the editor of the book, and the page numbers. Finally, for websites and online materials, it is customary to indicate what kind of source it is, the URL, and when the author accessed it. Examples of these are provided below in the three major styles. Notice that there are some slight differences, but much of the same information is included in each. The references in this example include:

1. A book written by Frank Ericson called "Coming Home," published by Tohoku Publishers in Sendai, Japan in 2014
2. An article written by Joshua Winterhalter called "Exploring how to cite papers in three styles," published in 2017 in volume 3, issue 7 of a journal called "The Journal of Educational Inception" on pages 113 to 127
3. A book chapter written by Taro Yamada and Hikari Sato called "Exploring the possibilities of nanorobots for cancer treatment" in the book "Innovations in Medical Technology" on pages 248 to 287. The book was edited by Steven Eldritch and published in New York by the Routledge Publishing Company in 2019.
4. An Internet site called "How to Succeed in Business" written by John Eagle, which was created on January 14th, 2019 and accessed on May 7th, 2020. The URL is www.fakewebsite.com/dontclickonthis.

APA Style

Ericson, F. (2014). *Coming home.* Tohoku Publishers.

Winterhalter, J. (2017). Exploring how to cite papers in three styles. *The Journal of Educational Inception, 3*(7), 113–127.

Yamada, T., & Sato, H. (2019). Exploring the possibilities of nanorobots for cancer treatment. In S. Eldritch (Ed.), *Innovations in Medical Technology* (pp. 248–287). Routledge.

Eagle, J. (2019, January 14). *How to succeed in business.* Retrieved from www.fakewebsite.com/dontclickonthis.

MLA Style

Ericson, Frank. *Coming Home.* Sendai, Tohoku Publishers, 2014.

Winterhalter, Joshua. "Exploring How to Cite Papers in Three Styles." *The Journal of Educational Inception,* vol. 3, no. 7, 2017, pp. 113–127.

Yamada, Taro, and Hikari Sato. "Exploring the possibilities of nanorobots for cancer treatment." *Innovations in Medical Technology,* edited by Steven Eldritch, Routledge, 2019, pp. 248–287.

Eagle, John. *How to Succeed in Business.* 14 January 2019, www.fakewebsite.com/dontclickonthis. Accessed 7 May 2020.

Chicago Style

Ericson, Frank. *Coming Home.* Sendai: Tohoku Publishers, 2014.

Winterhalter, Joshua. "Exploring How to Cite Papers in Three Styles." *The Journal of Educational Inception* 3, no. 7 (2017): 113-127.

Yamada, Taro and Hikari Sato. "Exploring the Possibilities of Nanorobots for Cancer Treatment." In *Innovations in Medical Technology,* edited by Steven Eldritch 248–287. New York: Routledge, 2019.

Eagle, John. "How to Succeed in Business." Last modified January 14, 2019, www.fakewebsite.com/dontclickonthis.

Example of Citing and Referencing in Use

Read the paragraph below and the references that come after it. Notice that both direct and indirect quotations are used and appear appropriately as in-text citations. The references in this example are given in APA format and therefore follow the guidelines given in this chapter, but they might be slightly different from the references used in other journals or books, depending on these publications' standards and regulations.

Many English as a Second Language students find citations challenging. They may not understand that, "If you don't cite the words of an author, you will be charged with plagiarism, which will result in a zero grade for the paper, and possibly expulsion from the university" (Collins, 2009, p.21). Many students are confused about using citations in their academic papers, and some research has shown that 55% of university students in the UK did not know how to correctly write citations (O'Leary & O'Malley, 2017). Teachers at universities are now trying to incorporate academic English writing courses into their curricula. A study by Barry (2020) showed that these courses have had a positive effect on the ability of students to produce essays that incorporate correct citations and references.

References

Collins, M. (2007). *Academic English*. Zoom Publishing.

O'Leary, J., & O'Malley, N. (2017). Citing properly. In J. Smith (Ed.), *Learning About Quotations* (pp. 12-48). Carlow University Press.

Barry, K. (2020). The state of academic writing. *Journal of Second Language Writing, 33*(4), 37-51.

C3 Presentation Preparation

The ability to give presentations is an essential academic skill that is necessary for reporting research findings and providing important information to an audience. In order to give a good presentation, the first and most critical step is preparation, which includes writing a proper script, designing visual aids, and practicing. Learning to prepare for an academic presentation will be important at Tohoku University because students will often be asked to give presentations to demonstrate knowledge in classes and to report the results of their experiments in laboratories. If the presentation is poorly organized, lacks engaging visuals, or has not been practiced, audiences will be confused about the content and bored.

What to Know about Presentation Preparation

There are eight essential steps for preparing a presentation: choosing a topic, outlining the main points and supporting evidence, researching the topic, writing a script, designing the visuals, understanding the setting, practicing the presentation, and preparing for questions and answers. Students must first be aware of what information is expected in the introduction, body and conclusion sections of a presentation (see Chapter C1) and then follow the below steps in order to prepare properly for a presentation.

Choosing a Topic

The first step in choosing a topic is to think carefully about the purpose of the presentation. In some cases, the topic will be decided by the purpose. For example, if the purpose of the presentation is to report research results, then the topic must be about the research in general. However, some classes allow students to research any area of their own interest. In this case, it is important to select a topic that is not too broad but also not too narrow. Even if the purpose of the presentation dictates a particular topic, students must still think about the scope of the presentation and the range of information to give. For example, if a student must report the results of their research, they should think about who the audience is and prepare an appropriate amount of background information. If the audience is other students in their laboratory who have some knowledge of the research project, then it is safe to assume that most of the listeners will be familiar with the research and will not need to be provided with extensive detail about previous studies. However, if the student is going to talk about the same research results to a group of non-experts, a more detailed explanation of the project will be required.

Outlining the Main Points and Supporting Evidence

After the topic and scope of the presentation have been defined, an outline of the main ideas and supporting evidence should be created. First, identify the main points that must be discussed in the presentation and try to reduce each to a simple phrase. For example, a main point should not be written as "talking about how solar energy helps the environment in many ways," but rather "environmental impacts of solar energy." Next, brainstorm ideas for supporting details and evidence for each main point and then organize them into notes (see Chapter B1.2). If a paper written in the Introduction–Body–Conclusion format is going to be presented, the main points and supporting evidence should already be clear.

Researching the Topic

Depending on the topic, scope, and purpose of the presentation, background research might be required to allow the presenter to speak competently. As discussed in Chapter C2, background research includes finding credible sources and taking notes about where they were found. Relevant details and important information should be added to the outline notes, and proper references should be included (see Chapter C2). In addition to searching for supporting evidence, remember to find appropriate definitions for technical terms and background information that will help the listeners to understand the topic in general.

Writing a Script

It is not a good idea to try to give a presentation without creating a script. Although it is generally not recommended to simply read from a script during the actual presentation, writing one helps presenters to organize their thoughts and plan their presentation appropriately. In addition, it is important to make the script as easy for listeners to understand as possible, which means that it should be well organized and use simple language.

The Introduction–Body–Conclusion format presented in Chapter C1 should be followed when creating presentation scripts to ensure that the presentation is well organized. The introduction should get the audience's attention and explain necessary background information so that they can understand the purpose of the presentation. The body sections should provide the details and evidence of the presentation and should be divided clearly, with one main idea per section. Finally, the conclusion should repeat the important information given in each section and end with a statement that moves the audience to reflect on the presentation or take action.

Presentation scripts should also use simple language, and therefore it is important to consider the differences between written and spoken English. Specifically, written English uses longer sentences than spoken English. In written texts long sentences are not problematic because readers can stop and re-read sections as many times as they like. However, when giving a presentation, listeners must be able to follow the speaker in real time. If the sentences are too long, listeners will be unable to process them, especially if there are mistakes or difficult vocabulary. Therefore, try to limit presentation sentences to around three to four clauses at most. In addition, written English tends to include many words of Latin or Greek origin (see Chapter

A1.1), which are longer and considered more difficult to process than simple English words. Thus, when writing a presentation script, try to use the simplest words possible and consider replacing words of Latinate origin with phrasal verbs (see Chapter B1.4). For example, "Extremely acidic substances can disintegrate bio-organic mass" could be replaced with "Strong acids can break down living tissue," which contains simpler words and is easier to understand.

Designing the Visuals

Most presentations contain visual aids, which are intended to enhance the message, make data clearer, and keep the audience's interest. Types of visual aids include graphs, charts, diagrams, summaries, photographs, video clips, handouts, and props. In academic presentations, it is common to use slideshow applications and a projector to show the visuals. When creating slides for a presentation, ensure that they strengthen the message and do not detract from it. Specifically, slides should add useful new information or summarize the message efficiently, but should not add irrelevant information or images that will distract the audience. For example, if a student is presenting about the difference in two companies' sales, a bar graph or pie chart can help an audience understand how big the difference is, but pictures of the speaker's vacation will only confuse the audience and shift focus from the important information. Furthermore, slides should be made as simple as possible by limiting the contents of each slide to no more than two pieces of key information, using images instead of text wherever possible, and not using full sentences. Consider the following slides. Notice that the first one is nearly impossible to read and difficult to understand. The second slide uses text but only mentions the key points, which makes it easier to understand. The third slide uses an image instead of text, making it the best slide of all.

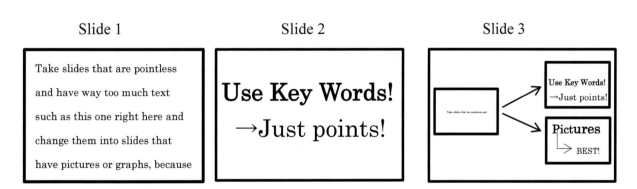

Slide 1   Slide 2   Slide 3

Finally, using color and design to make the slides or other visual aids interesting can help get the audience's attention. While there is no single rule for doing this, it is often a good idea to use a common color scheme throughout the presentation and place images and text in easily visible and sensibly distributed on the slides.

Understanding the Setting

The next step in preparing for a presentation is being aware of the setting in which the presentation will be given and adjusting accordingly. Specifically, the speaker should find out whether a computer and projector will be available for their visuals, how long the presentation is expected to be, whether there will be a question-and-answer session, how large the room is, and how many people are expected to attend. The speaker should practice and adjust their script based on this information and make any other necessary preparations before the day of the presentation. For example, if the presentation will be given in a large room and the speaker is expected to use a microphone, it is a good idea for the speaker to practice with this in mind; and if the speaker is unsure whether there will be a computer available for use, it is a good idea for them to bring their own.

Practicing the Presentation

It is obvious when a speaker has not practiced giving their presentation, as they will usually pace themselves poorly, take long pauses in inappropriate places, and appear nervous. A well-rehearsed presentation will seem smooth and natural without the speaker having to read from a script. For the best outcome, speakers should practice by doing the following:

First, begin by reading the script aloud several times, marking words and phrases that are difficult to pronounce. As suggested in Chapter B2.3, reading the script into a voice recognition application can help identify problem areas for further practice. After practicing the pronunciation of these words and reading the script repeatedly, focus on improving fluency by timing how long it takes to read the script and then trying to read it faster several times. Next, create simple notecards with the main points and important supporting details written on them and use these instead of the script to give the presentation. Try doing this a few times while timing how long it takes; a speech recognition application can be used here as well. It is not a problem if the presentation does not mirror the script exactly, as long as the important information is still presented in a well-organized manner and with appropriate accuracy and fluency. Finally, check that the presentation can be given within the time allowed. If it is too long or short, adjust the script appropriately and continue practicing.

When the speaker is able to give the presentation in a clear and well-organized manner within the time limits and only using the notecards occasionally for assistance, they have practiced sufficiently. It is not recommended that speakers memorize their speech in full or read directly from a script or notecards during their actual presentation, as this makes the presentation sound unnatural and distracts the speaker, who must pay attention to the audience (see Chapter C4).

Preparing for Questions and Answers

Most presentations are followed by a question-and-answer session, in which the speaker is expected to answer the audience's questions. When answering audience questions, use the question–response skill discussed in Chapter B1.3. Also, be sure to use an appropriate level of politeness, as discussed in Chapter B2.2, but know that it is considered polite to thank audience members for their questions. Furthermore, do not despair if you do not understand a question or cannot answer it completely. If it is unclear what is being asked, simply ask for the question to be repeated. If this does not work, try rephrasing the question and asking if that is what the questioner meant. Moreover, be sure to have a good dialogue with audience members who ask questions. For example, consider asking "Does that answer your question?" or "Is that clear?" to ensure that they have understood the answer, and be considerate by giving the best answer possible. Remember that if you do not know the answer, "I'm sorry, I don't know" is an acceptable response. Finally, though it is impossible to predict every question that will be asked, it is a good idea to think about questions that might be asked and prepare answers to them. The answers to these questions can be prepared using the same procedure employed in practicing the presentation.

Example of Presentation Preparation in Use

Look at the examples of two different introductions for the same presentation. Notice that one is difficult to understand because it is not organized well and uses long sentences with too many difficult words. The other is much easier to understand because it follows the Introduction–Body–Conclusion principle of organization, uses shorter sentences, and contains simpler vocabulary. Furthermore, the difficult-to-understand introduction does not provide adequate background information, so it is unlikely that it was properly researched or outlined, whereas the easy-to-understand introduction likely was.

Difficult-to-Understand Introduction
The consideration of the possibility of extraterrestrial bio-organisms is essential to academic endeavors. Aquatic environments, carbon, and thermoregulation appropriate for life is what astrobiologists investigate exoplanets for. This is because these components are necessary for life in general. Therefore, this presentation discusses the trifecta of astrobiology such that you will better appreciate why funds are utilized for this pursuit versus other more practical, terrestrial concerns.

Easy-to-Understand Introduction
Have you ever wondered whether there is alien life on other planets? This question has been of great interest to scientists and everyday people for many years. That is why the study of astrobiology is so important. Astrobiology is a branch of science that looks for signs of life beyond Earth. However, astrobiologists do not search for alien monsters or human-like creatures. Instead, they seek out places where simple life forms such as bacteria could live, by trying to find planets that have the building blocks for life. Today, I will introduce the three things that scientists look for when trying to find life beyond Earth: water, carbon, and heat.

C4 Presentation Strategies

Presentation strategies refer to the skills and techniques used during a speech or presentation that help to make it clear and effective. Learning presentation strategies helps speakers to reduce their anxiety and develop their confidence. This not only makes presenting easier but also makes the delivery more engaging, which increases the likelihood of the audience appreciating the information and remembering it later. Therefore, these skills are important at Tohoku University when students give academic presentations in their classes and at research meetings and will also be useful after graduation, whether students become academics, researchers, or company employees.

What to Know about Presentation Strategies

There are three broad categories of presentation strategies: spoken language, body language, and visual language. The spoken language strategies included in this chapter are pronunciation and intonation, pace, volume, and tone. The body language strategies covered in this chapter are gestures, facial expressions, eye contact, movement, and posture. Finally, the visual language strategies in this chapter are content variety and physical appearance.

Spoken Language Strategies

The first spoken language strategy to be discussed is pronunciation and intonation. Of course, non-native speakers must be especially careful with the pronunciation of English in general and should practice before giving a presentation. The standard ways of using intonation should also be reviewed (see Chapter B2.3). However, intonation can also be used in special ways in speeches and presentations. Specifically, adding stress and length to words that are especially important in a presentation helps listeners to understand that these are key words that they should listen for. This will make the presentation clearer and easier to follow. In general, speakers should aim to give twice as much stress or length to important words and phrases spoken during a presentation than they might when having a conversation or discussion.

Pacing is also an important consideration during a speech or presentation. Finishing too quickly or not quickly enough will disrupt the question-and-answer session and/or the next presenter, so speakers should keep an eye on the clock while presenting so that they can ensure their pace is not too fast or too slow. Speakers who are nervous tend to talk too quickly, even when speaking in a second language, which makes their presentations difficult to follow and understand. One way to control pace is to focus on breathing. Tension in the stomach and chest leads to shallow breathing, which causes people to speak more quickly. Taking deep breaths and trying to breathe evenly can relax a speaker, giving them better control over the pace of their speech. Another way to control pace is to use pauses during the speech. These are best used just before or after important points or pieces of information, where the pause helps to signal that the surrounding words are significant while simultaneously giving the speaker the chance to stop and take a deep breath.

The volume of a speaker's voice is also critical to a good presentation. Of course, if they do not speak loudly enough, the audience will not be able to hear them, and they will not receive any of the information from the presentation. If no microphone is available, be sure to stand up straight, breathe deeply, and use the diaphragm (stomach muscles) to push air out when speaking. This will ensure that your voice travels throughout the room and that you are heard. If a microphone is available, still be sure to speak loudly enough and check that the audience can hear you by asking questions such as "Can everyone hear me alright?" or "Can you hear me in the back?" Finally, avoid making distracting noises, such as clicking a pen or tapping on the blackboard. Similarly, if the audience makes noise, for example when laughing or applauding, wait for it to subside before continuing.

The final speaking strategy is to use a good tone when speaking. This means that the speaker should be energetic and interested in what they are saying. Even if they are not really excited about the topic, they should try to fake enthusiasm, as lively speakers are more engaging and better able to capture the audience's attention. If a speaker lacks energy or enthusiasm, the audience will become disinterested, and they will likely not pay close attention to the presentation or remember it later.

Body Language Strategies

A speaker's body language sends a message to the audience about how serious and credible they are, how interesting the topic is, and where the important information in the presentation is. The first strategy that a speaker can employ to send an appropriate message through body language is the use of gestures. Unlike informal gestures used in conversation, gestures in presentations can be used to call attention to specific information. For example, pointing or waving during a particular sentence signals to the audience that it is especially important. Furthermore, gestures can be demonstrative and serve to illustrate a point for the audience. For example, if a speaker wants the audience to know that something is 30 centimeters long, they could gesture to show approximately how long 30 centimeters is, helping the audience to visualize what the speaker is talking about. Though using gestures in a presentation generally makes a positive impression on the audience, speakers should be aware of inadvertent gestures, or gestures that they make without thinking. Most inadvertent gestures, such as rubbing one's hands together, tapping one's foot, or rocking back and forth, are simply distracting and make a bad impression on the audience. Since inadvertent gestures usually occur when one is nervous, speakers who make too many of them during a presentation will be perceived by the audience as not confident, credible or serious about their topic.

Facial expressions can also help send messages to the audience. If a speaker does not make any facial expressions, it gives the impression that they are uninterested in the topic, which will lead the audience to become bored. Use of a range of facial expressions that align with what is being spoken about will engage the audience and increase the impact of the presentation. For example, a surprised or shocked expression should be used with surprising facts, and a smile should be used when discussing happy or humorous moments. Speakers can practice the use of facial expressions by giving their speech in front of a mirror before the day of the presentation.

One of the most important components of body language strategy is eye contact. It is important for speakers to meet the eyes of the audience members for short periods of time in order to connect with them. This connection engages the audience, making them feel that they must pay close attention to the presentation. If a speaker does not make any eye contact with the audience and only looks at their slides, their script, or the chalkboard, the presentation quickly becomes boring, which decreases the likelihood of the audience listening carefully or remembering the information later. This is why it is not recommended to simply read a speech or presentation from a script. Furthermore, good use of eye contact gives the speaker clues about the audience's reactions. If the audience seems uninterested, the speaker may consider using more gestures or facial expressions. Similarly, if the audience seems confused, it is a clue that the speaker should speak more slowly or explain a point again or more carefully. Speakers who are too nervous or embarrassed to make eye contact can try looking just above the heads of the audience or dividing the room into zones and looking at each zone for just a few seconds.

Another way in which body language strategies can make a presentation more engaging is adding movement. For one, if a speaker moves around the room or stage, it can add excitement and variety. However, speakers can also make movements when introducing important information to signal to the audience that the information is significant. For example, a speaker could return to the left side of the stage every time they introduce a new main point, which would help the audience to understand when the speaker is transitioning between topics. However, be aware that too much movement becomes distracting. Aim for a small amount of movement in the room or on the stage about once every minute.

Finally, posture (how the speaker stands) can also be an important body language strategy when giving presentations and speeches. Speakers should avoid looking down, shrinking their bodies, or shifting from side to side. These movements make the speaker look nervous, which conveys to the audience that the speaker is not confident or credible. Speakers who are naturally nervous should be aware of this and make an effort to stand up straight with their weight evenly distributed on their feet and their shoulders back. Furthermore, standing up straight helps speakers to use their diaphragm muscles and speak more loudly and clearly. Finally, speakers should be aware of their own nervous habits and try to repress them. For example, if a speaker knows that their mouth tends to become dry, they can be sure to have a bottle of water nearby.

Visual Language Strategies

The visual language of a presentation refers to what the audience can see and what kind of message it sends to the audience. The first thing to consider here is how much variety there is in the visual content. When giving a presentation, it is more engaging to call the audience's attention to a variety of things. For example, sometimes it is best for the speaker to be the focus of the presentation, but looking only at a single person becomes boring very quickly. At appropriate times, the speaker should ask the audience to look at a visual aid, such as a chart, a handout or a particular gesture. If the speaker uses only one type of visual aid, never moves to a different area of the stage, or uses only one type of gesture, the audience will become disengaged and stop paying attention. Therefore, it is important to not only plan for a variety of visual aids but to remember to use the different types of body language strategies and move the audience's attention to various places while speaking.

The final aspect to consider when giving a presentation is physical appearance. Of course, every person looks different, and this chapter does not suggest any drastic changes, such as losing weight or coloring one's hair. However, speakers should do their best to look their best when giving a presentation by dressing appropriately and grooming adequately. Regardless of whether or not it is right, most people form first impressions quickly and rarely change their opinions. Therefore, it is important to look professional from the beginning. Wearing appropriate clothing will send the message that the speaker is competent and knowledgeable. Similarly, improper grooming can lead to a strange appearance that is distracting to the audience and might cause them to miss important information in the presentation.

Example of Presentation Strategies in Use

Here is a script for an example presentation. Watch the same presentation given two times, once with bad use of presentation strategies and once with good use of presentation strategies. Notice how in the bad version the speaker's monotone voice is boring, their body language is flat, and the visual language sends the message that the speaker is not confident in what he is saying. In contrast, the good version makes good use of pace, volume, and tone to make the presentation sound more exciting; the speaker's body language is engaging; and the visual language makes a good impression. For these reasons, the second version of the presentation is much better.

Script

Most people are interested in knowing about the planets of our solar system, but scientists have actually discovered many planets outside of the solar system. These planets are called exoplanets, and they are very interesting because there are so many of them and they differ greatly! As of August 1, 2020, scientists have confirmed the existence of 4,301 exoplanets. The smallest is only about twice the size of the Moon, while the largest may be 90 times larger than Jupiter. However, despite how interesting they are, scientists are struggling to obtain funding to research exoplanets in more detail. In today's presentation, I want to convince you that studying exoplanets is important because it advances technology, educates us about life on Earth, and helps us to prepare for threats from space.

Script

編 集
Ryan Spring

執 筆
Barry Kavanagh
Yoshio Kitahara
Richard Meres
Shizuka Sakurai
Vincent Scura
Ryan Spring
Joseph Stavoy
Shuichi Takebayashi

表紙デザイン
Nami Ogata

Pathways to Academic English 2021

©Institute for Excellence in Higher Education, Tohoku University 2021

2021 年 3 月 1 日　　初版第 1 刷発行
2021 年 8 月 1 日　　初版第 2 刷発行

編　者／東北大学高度教養教育・学生支援機構
発行者／関　内　　隆
発行所／東北大学出版会
　　　　〒980-8577　仙台市青葉区片平 2-1-1
　　　　TEL：022-214-2777　FAX：022-214-2778
　　　　https://www.tups.jp/　E-mail：info@tups.jp
印　刷／東北大学生活協同組合
　　　　〒980-0845　仙台市青葉区荒巻字青葉 468-1
　　　　東北大学みどり厚生会館内 2 階
　　　　TEL：022-262-8022

ISBN 978-4-86163-353-9　C3082